CHAMPIONS OF THE KING

Other books by Sally Pierson Dillon:

War of the Ages Series:

Survivors of the Dark Rebellion
Exile of the Chosen
Victory of the Warrior King
Champions of the King
War of the Invisibles

Little Hearts for Jesus
Hugs From Jesus
Michael Asks Why (Pacific Press)

To order, call **1-800-765-6955.**

Visit us at www.reviewandherald.com for information on other Review and Herald® products.

CHAMPIONS OF THE KING

THE STORY OF
THE APOSTLES

SALLY PIERSON DILLON

REVIEW AND HERALD® PUBLISHING ASSOCIATION
Since 1861 | www.reviewandherald.com

The author assumes full responsibility for the accuracy of all facts and
quotations as cited in this book.

Texts credited to Message are from *The Message.* Copyright © 1993, 1994,
1995, 1996, 2000, 2001, 2002. Used by permission of NavPress Publishing Group.
Scriptures credited to NCV are quoted from *The Holy Bible, New Century
Version,* copyright © 1987, 1988, 1991 by Word Publishing, Dallas, Texas
75039. Used by permission.

This book was
Edited by Gerald Wheeler
Designed by Trent Truman
Cover art by Greg and Tim Hildebrandt
Electronic makeup by Shirley M. Bolivar
Typeset: Berkeley Book 12/16

PRINTED IN U.S.A.

12 11 10 09 08   6 5 4 3 2

R&H Cataloging Service
Dillon, Sally Pierson, 1959-2007.
     Champions of the king.

     1. Bible. N.T.—History—Juvenile works.   I. Title.

                    221.09

ISBN 978-0-8280-1704-6

# Dedication

To my husband, Bruce, who has been my long-term cheerleader and who connived with Penny Wheeler to get me to my first writers' conference at the Review and Herald Publishing Association.

With great appreciation for the editors of Guide magazine, especially Jeannette Johnson and Randy Fishell, without whose encouragement and opportunities for maturing I might still be the eager wannabe writer scrawling reams of stuff that I never let anyone read—as I was doing when they met me.

And to Gerald Wheeler for walking me through four of these five books, keeping my history and theology correct and properly expressed.

You are all precious people without whom these books would not exist.

Main Characters

antonia Daughter of a Roman centurion staying at the Antonia Fortress in Jerusalem

elihu Son of Malchus, personal servant of the high priest, now helping take over his father's tasks

sulimon Servant to the treasurer of the queen mother of Ethiopia, returning home from Jerusalem

thaddeus The son of a former demoniac of Gadera, now part of a family of new believers helping run his uncle's inn in Damascus, Syria

portia Daughter of Antonia—lives in Caesarea

jonathan Son of Doud (a leper Jesus healed) and Martha of Bethany

vesta Young daughter of the jailer in the city of Philippi

dion Son of an alcoholic father who sells the boy as a slave (a tentmaker named Aquilla then purchases him)

lucas A young silversmith's apprentice until the boy has to choose between his job and family or being a believer like his friend Dion

matteo Son of a ship's captain who meets an unusual prisoner being transported to Rome under a military guard

Aптoпiа

(Jerusalem—Antonia Fortress)

ntonia let out a loud sigh and turned away from the window.

"What is it?" Portia, the stately wife of Pilate, governor of Judea, asked her.

"I'm sorry," the girl said with a start. "I didn't realize anybody was in here with me."

The woman smiled. "I know."

"I don't mean to sound ungrateful," Antonia said. "You have been so good to me here. I know my father couldn't leave me in Capernaum by myself. And he certainly couldn't keep me down in the barracks with the soldiers."

"You've been a pleasure to have here," Portia interrupted. "Pilate and I never had any children, and I have really enjoyed your company."

"And I yours. But I've been here a really long time."

"You're homesick, aren't you?" Portia questioned.

The girl sighed again. "I am. When Father and I came here I thought we were just staying for the Passover."

"Yes, my husband wanted extra reinforcements in case of rioting during the Passover celebration. Remember, there was a lot of political unrest."

Antonia shuddered. She still had nightmares about the crucifixion. While the daughter of a soldier sometimes encountered crucifixions, this one had been different. It had been the crucifixion of Yeshua of Nazareth, the one who had healed Petronius, her beloved elderly servant who had cared for her all her life. This was Yeshua who had restored Deborah after she had died. The girl had been Antonia's playmate. Suddenly she smiled to herself as she thought of how she certainly could never have Deborah visit her here in the heavily guarded Antonio Fortress that housed Pilate's palatial dwelling. But then the Jewish girl would never come inside the home of a Gentile anyway. And all of their friendship and adventures had to take place outside in the market, in the courtyards, and by the community well.

A thought made her chuckle to herself. She was the daughter of a Roman centurion and someone whom everyone would consider really stooping way below her social class to be friends with a young Hebrew girl in an occupied territory, and yet the Hebrew girl refused to enter *Antonia's* home. How could they ever have been friends in the first place? Antonia shook her head. *Who cares?* she thought. *I just wish I could go home and see her again.*

"Has Pilate mentioned anything about letting Father go home?" she asked, turning back to Portia. "Do you know when we might go back? It's been months!"

"It has been months," the woman agreed. She put her arm around the homesick girl. "Pilate has a great deal of respect for your father. Your father is unusual in that he is well respected by not only his own men, but also many of the Jews."

Antonia understood how unusual that was. The people of Palestine hated Romans in general—at least according to Deborah. Yet her father had been extremely kind to them and treated them with respect, which was unusual for anyone in an occupying army.

"Because of your father's relationships and his skills with these unruly Judeans," Portia continued, "he's been very valuable to my husband here in Jerusalem. It seems that the political unrest of the Passover is not over yet. Pilate would like him to remain here in Jerusalem. In fact, my husband is considering posting him permanently at the Antonio Fortress."

"Here?" the girl exclaimed in horror. "Here?"

The woman nodded. "It's still under discussion, but it would appear to be a very wise move on Pilate's part."

"But what would I do? What about me?"

"Antonia," Portia said gently, "have you ever thought about your future and what you might like to do with your life?"

She stared at the older woman. "You mean like getting married and having a family?"

"Yes. Like that."

"No, I hadn't thought about it. I always figured—Father always said—someday we would go back to Rome. And I guess I thought I would marry someone there someday."

"Well," Portia continued, "it may be that if my husband reassigns your father to the Antonio Fortress here, it would be a good time for a marriage for you. You obviously can't live in the barracks, and it would be best for your father to be there with his men. I believe Pilate is planning many additional responsibilities for him. It will be a great honor. But keeping a single daughter here would be most difficult. You are of marriageable age. And while your father will not be able to take you back to Rome to find you a husband, there are some very attractive Romans here."

Antonia shuddered. "We've never really talked about this." She thought a moment. "What if I don't want to get married?"

Portia smiled. "None of us *want* to get married exactly when our parents start to arrange it. It's just something that is part of life. Your father has spoken to Pilate about it, and I will help them choose someone. We'll make sure we get someone who's kind to you and who is a good husband. Someone who has a good position and can provide well for you."

"Thank you," Antonia managed to say before bursting into tears.

Portia quietly slipped from the room. She remembered several years ago sobbing into her pillow at the idea of marrying Pilate, and yet it had not been so bad. Wasn't this how life went for everyone, with the only difference that some girls wound up with unkind men or husbands without any money? And she would make sure that Antonia would not have to worry about either.

The following morning Antonia joined Portia for breakfast, and, while the centurion's daughter smiled and tried to be pleasant, Portia noticed the red swollen eyes and the puffy face.

After the meal Portia said, "Come with me. I know something that you might enjoy. It will certainly distract you for a little while."

She led Antonia to a high point on the fortress wall, then motioned to a soldier who placed a wooden box on the ground. Portia stepped up on to it and pulled Antonia up with her. "Look right down there," she said.

Antonia caught her breath sharply. They were able to gaze down into the courtyard of the Jewish Temple.

"You can see everything that goes on from up here," the woman explained. "It probably infuriates the Jews, but it's very interesting."

"Look," the girl exclaimed. "Those men in the corner there with all the people. Weren't they with Yeshua of Nazareth?"

"Yes, they were. That group calls itself the believers. They are the followers of Yeshua. Every day more join them."

"Are they safe there in the Temple in front of the priests?"

Portia laughed. "Not particularly. Their presence makes the priests furious, but right now the Temple rulers are afraid to do anything because of the great popularity of the group's leaders. The number of Yeshua followers increases every day, and the high priest and Jewish Sanhedrin don't know what to do. They keep asking my husband to act, but of course he's hardly going to interfere when nobody's breaking any laws."

Antonia suddenly pointed. "Look! They're bringing a person in on a bed. Why?"

"Word is," Portia explained, "that the followers of Yeshua are able to perform miracles just as He did. They deny that claim and say that it is just the Spirit of Yeshua, who is still here who is doing the miracles. Whatever people want to believe, apparently they are being healed. Watch this."

Sure enough, one of the leaders touched the person on the stretcher, and the individual jumped up and started leaping and praising God.

"Does it happen often?" Antonia asked.

"Yes, every day. I watch from here a lot. Sometimes the miracles apparently happen from just being touched by Peter's shadow as he walks by—Peter is the burly one there. See those people down there with their handkerchiefs, holding them up to him? They believe that if he touches them and they take them home to their sick ones, they are healed too."

"And are they?" the girl asked.

"According to all of our spies and agents, it's true. Of course, some people will never believe it unless they actually see it themselves. But I've witnessed enough from up here that I believe it's likely to be true."

"That is wonderful," Antonia exclaimed. "So the power of Yeshua and His Spirit is still here, even if His body is not."

"Yes, they say He was taken up to heaven in the clouds. Of course, that may be just a story, but who knows? No one has seen Him since then."

"I believe it," Antonia declared. "Everything else the believers have said about Him is true."

"Yes, you would make a good believer."

The girl smiled. "Really? I would love to be one of His followers."

"Well, you can't," Portia announced. "Look at where they meet. You know what happens to any Gentiles who go inside of there apart from the soldiers sent in to take care of uprisings and such?"

Antonia sighed. "Yes, Gentiles are not allowed inside the Temple courts on pain of execution."

"Right. Yeshua's followers meet in there. They don't want people like us. We're not allowed to be believers. It's just for Jews."

"But Yeshua healed my servant Petronius," the girl frowned, "and he's not a Jew."

Portia shrugged. "Yeshua may have had different ideas, but His followers are pretty restricted just to Jews, so you might as well get married and make a good life for yourself. As fascinating as this is, it's not something we're allowed to be a part of."

"I suppose you're right," Antonia said sadly. "Do you know who my father has in mind?"

"I do," Portia replied, her eyes twinkling. "Would you like to hear about him? Come on, let's go back inside."

They walked back into the cool interior of the fortress. The two women stretched out on the couches in Portia's elegant chamber.

"So tell me about my future husband," Antonia said, trying to sound cheerful.

"Well, his name is Cornelius, and he is a Roman from Italy like your father. A centurion, he is highly respected and head of an elite group. All of his soldiers are also Romans from Italy. They're known as the Italian Band."

"Is he here in Jerusalem?"

"No, he's stationed in Caesarea. You know it is the military headquarters for this area. Cornelius had wanted a woman from Italy, also, and had figured he would just have to wait to marry until he was stationed there again. However, he will be delighted to have you."

For a moment Antonia wondered how pleased Cornelius actually would be about the situation. Perhaps he wasn't going to be any more excited about having an arranged marriage than she was. But she said nothing.

"Anyway," Portia continued, "we've arranged for a wedding in two weeks."

"Two weeks!"

"Well, of course. As Romans we do things at our convenience. We aren't bound by those rules the Jews here use in which you have to wait a whole year from your betrothal before you can go live with your husband. Two weeks isn't long, but we can put together an amazing celebration in that time."

"Yes, I'm sure you can," the girl said, her mind spinning. Only two weeks!

Antonia found it distracting to spend more and more time standing on her box by the wall watching the Yeshua believers in the Temple courtyard. Sometimes she felt she could almost hear what was going on. Other times she had to imagine from the way people acted.

I hovered gently near her, watching her soaking up every bit of believer culture that she could from the top of the wall. The walls in the courtyard were thick with guardians, and while very little seemed to be going on to the human eye, the battle was raging amongst the rest of us.

"Oh, no," Antonia gasped. She watched as Temple guards charged into the believers, pushing them out of the way, grabbing Peter and John and dragging them toward the gate closest to the fortress. "What are they doing?" she asked a soldier on the wall near her.

"Apparently they're arresting those two."

"But why?"

"Who knows? They're Jews, touchy at best, and I imagine that the priests and those who think they have authority feel threatened by these men."

It isn't that different from the problems Yeshua had with them, Antonia thought to herself. She hurried inside. Perhaps she could find Portia. Maybe she could even get a message to her father. Surely the Jewish authorities wouldn't do anything to the men! At least not anything bad!

"We can't do anything about it," Portia explained when the girl told her what had happened. "This is a time when we need to mind our own business."

"But what will they do to them?"

"I don't know. The last time they just gave them a stern warning and let them go. But we really must not get involved unless there is a major crisis."

"This is a major crisis," Antonia protested.

Portia took the girl's hands. "No, it isn't. You are not a Jew. Nor are you even a believer. They wouldn't even let you be in their group. So you must let them settle this themselves. If the Romans intervened every time there was a conflict among the Jews, they would hate us even more than they do now. Let's just wait and see what happens."

"But we've already involved. They're in our prison."

"You have to let this go."

Slowly Antonia walked back to her quarters. She had never been so unhappy.

When the servant girl brought her breakfast she snapped at her and sent her scurrying back to the kitchen with her food untouched. As she lay on her bed and stared at the wall, she whispered, "God of Yeshua of Nazareth, why did You heal Petronius? Why were You so kind to us if You don't want anyone but Jews for believers? Is that the way You feel, or is that just what they believe?

And if You can do all of these miracles, healing all of these people down there, couldn't You do something about my life? I don't want to be made into a Jew. I like being a Roman. But I don't want to marry Cornelius and live a pagan Roman life. I want to be a believer. Is there anything You can do about that? Assuming, of course, that You want Roman believers." Then the tears began to flow, and she said nothing more to the God of Yeshua. And it seemed that He wasn't going to say anything to her, either.

Suddenly a blinding light made her squeeze her eyes shut. "Come on, get up," Portia said after whipping open the curtains. "It's hours after you're usually awake. What's the problem today? Are you ill?"

Antonia shook her head. "Well, I don't feel very well, but I don't think I'm sick."

"H'mm, I see the problem. Here, put this on. There's something I want to show you."

"I—I can't go out like this. I'm not bathed or dressed or any-thing yet."

"Well, whose fault is that?" Portia handed her a garment. "Put this on and tie the belt. We're going out to the wall."

"I don't want to go out there anymore," the girl wailed.

"Yes, you do. Come and see." She dragged Antonia by the hand.

"Have you heard when their trial is supposed to be?"

"The Sanhedrin is meeting this morning to decide their fate."

"Then why are you dragging me out here?"

"There's something I want you to see. Here, get up on the box."

Slowly Antonia climbed up and looked down into the Temple. Then she caught her breath sharply and clapped her hand over her mouth. "But how can they have their trial when they're here?"

"Well," Portia said, "I don't think the Sanhedrin knows that they're here. The elders are all heading into the main chamber, where they're planning to have the trial."

They both started giggling.

"Oh, that's funny. They're going to be so angry."

That evening as they were sharing dinner with Pilate in his private quarters Portia and Antonia told him what they had seen.

"It was so funny," Portia laughed. "All these old graybeards lining up and entering the apartments of Annas for their Sanhedrin meeting and then sending for the prisoners when the men were actually sitting in the courtyard preaching away as always."

Pilate remained expressionless.

"Well, what's the matter? Don't you think it's funny?" his wife asked.

"No. It would be if it were only the graybeards involved, but these believers and their God also made a fool of me and my guards and the fortress. How did they get out of our dungeon? All the guards were still there. The doors were still locked. The chains were still in place. Nothing had moved. How do you take a man's foot out of a manacle without breaking the lock on it? You couldn't do it without amputating his foot. And yet these men were clearly all in one piece out in the courtyard. My soldiers still don't understand how it happened."

Portia and Antonia were quiet. Pilate was right—it wasn't funny. And guards who allowed prisoners to escape usually faced execution. They finished eating in silence.

"So it's just about time for your wedding," Pilate said to Antonia afterward. "Are you getting excited?"

Portia shot him a warning look.

"Umm, I guess so," the girl managed to reply. "So many things have been happening that I haven't really been able to give it much thought."

"H'mm," Pilate said. "Well, there'll be time to think about it later. Now if you two will excuse me, I still have some things to do this evening."

Later Portia walked out to the wall where Antonia was standing on her box watching. "You've been out here a long time," she said. "Is there something interesting going on?"

"I'm trying to figure out what they're doing. They seem to be appointing people for something. See those seven men down there? The believers chose them for something. The main leaders laid their hands on the men's heads and then seemed to be praying for a long time. Do you have any idea what they're up to?"

Portia looked down. "I'm afraid not. Those seven there?"

"Yes," Antonia replied, pointing.

"They look a little younger than the preachers," Portia observed.

"And ever since whatever the ceremony was they've been passing food out to the widows and the children over on that side. I'm not sure what it was they were selected to do, but they haven't done any preaching."

"It's hard to tell when we can't hear much from up here," Portia said. "Maybe the preachers appointed them to pass the food out so that they could spend their time speaking instead."

Antonia thought a moment. "That could be, because they get interrupted a lot, not only with trying to pass out food or donated money, but also people seem to come to them to complain about things. At least that's what I guess they're doing when they're waving their arms and such."

"Well, if I were one of those preachers, I think I would appoint someone to handle the complaints and food distribution so that I could get on with what I really needed to do."

"That makes sense," Antonia decided. "I'll keep watching and see if the believers are as smart as you are."

Portia laughed. "Don't stand out here in the hot sun all day. You'll get heatstroke. Besides, you need to spend at least some time soaking in scented oils and getting ready for the wedding."

The girl frowned. "Well, the wedding's not coming up for several days yet," she protested.

Pilate's wife rolled her eyes. "That's the problem with being raised by your father and an elderly servant in this forsaken country. If you were in Rome, you would have been soaking in scented oils every day for months before your wedding."

"Well, then it's a good thing I'm not in Rome. I don't think I could stand that. Bathing and being clean should be enough."

"Well, please allow me to civilize you for at least a week before you marry Cornelius. I don't want him to think that I have fixed him up with a wild woman."

"All right, I'm coming. I'll soak in whatever horrible concoction you have in there as long as you promise to let me bathe and wash it off afterward."

Portia threw up her hands. "And then what would be the point?" And the two went back into the palace laughing.

* * *

Shouting filled the air. Antonia jumped up and ran to her window. Unable to see anything, she hurried out to the spot on the wall where she and Portia often viewed the Temple courtyard. A mob of angry graybeards was dragging someone out the gate.

Portia joined her. "Quickly," she said, "down here. At the other end of the fortress we can see beyond the gate. That seems to be where they're going."

The sheep gate was right next to a large pool where the Levites bathed the animals designated for sacrifice. It wasn't the best smelling place. Farther over was a beautiful pool, much cleaner and better smelling, for humans, called the Pool of Bethesda. It had tall colonnades to shelter the disabled people who lay around it.

"Yeshua of Nazareth healed one of them once," Portia commented, indicating the rows of invalids. "I was watching from up here that day."

"You got to see it?" Antonia asked excitedly.

"I did. The man He healed had been lying there the whole time Pilate and I had been coming to Jerusalem. After Jesus cured the invalid I saw him walking. Rolling up his mat, he headed down into the city. He really was healed."

"Just like Petronius," Antonia said. She studied the commotion below. "Who do they have there?"

By this time the mob had thrown the person on the ground and were forming a circle around him.

"I recognize him," Antonia exclaimed. "He's one of the ones chosen last week."

"He's been passing out food to the widows." Pilate's voice behind them made them jump. "Apparently he's tried his hand at preaching, too, and it's gotten him into a lot of trouble."

"We haven't seen him preaching," Portia said, turning to her husband and slipping her hand into his.

"Well, my sources say that he didn't until they trumped up some false charges and pulled him in front of the Sanhedrin. Someone wants to get rid of him."

"Well, if they were false, then wasn't he able to prove his innocence?"

Pilate seemed irritable. "You know how these Jews are."

"So what are they going to do?" Antonia questioned.

But she really hadn't needed to ask. It was becoming obvious. The mob began picking up stones. The young man backed away from it. The crowd parted a little until he was against the city wall. Then they started hurling the rocks.

"They're stoning him," Antonia said numbly. "Why are they killing him?"

"Apparently for blasphemy," Pilate said.

"Do something," Portia demanded. "It's illegal for them to execute anybody without your permission. Do something!"

Pilate turned his back to the grizzly scene. "I see nothing."

"That's not true! Have they got you so intimidated that you refuse to use your own authority?" his wife screamed. "Are you so afraid of those priests that you can't even be the governor?"

Pilate turned in anger and grabbed her roughly by the arm. "If you were anyone else—anyone else in this entire empire—I would have you executed for that!"

Tears welled up in Portia's eyes. She touched his cheek. "My *carus*," she said. "What have they done to you?"

"Don't *carus* me!" he snapped.

Portia burst into tears, and Pilate put both arms around her. The soldier standing near them on the wall kept his eyes firmly fixed on the ground, but uncomfortably shifted his weight from one foot to the other.

In horror Antonia watched the execution continue.

The young man crumpled to his knees now and shouted, his words echoing off the city wall, "I can see the heavens opening. I can see Yeshua on the right hand of God."

Antonia put her hands up to her temples. Her head was throbbing. "Yeshua," she said. "I want the heavens to open. I want to see You too."

Suddenly all the noise around her became far away. It was as if she was seeing things through a long, dark tunnel before the darkness swallowed her up and she fell to the pavement with a heavy thud.

When Antonia awoke she was aware only of a terrible headache, but as her eyes focused she realized there was someone in the room with her.

"Father," she cried, "I've missed you terribly."

The centurion reached out his hand and held hers. "I was really worried about you. What happened?"

His daughter rubbed her head. "Uh, I'm not sure."

"Ah. The governor had his private physicians examine you."

"Have I got some terrible illness so I won't have to marry Cornelius now?" she asked.

Her father chuckled. "No. Did you want some terrible illness?"
Antonia looked down.

"The doctor said that you were fine, but that you looked as if
you had not been sleeping or eating well lately."

She nodded. "It's true. I've been homesick for Capernaum."

"The governor's wife has already told me this, but there's not
much I can do about that. I've been asked to take over the garrison
here and be in charge of the men who guard the fortress. Not only
is it a great honor; it's not a promotion that I'm allowed to refuse."

"I know," she said, staring at the floor.

"Look," he said, "this weekend you're going to be married.
You'll have a whole new life. As long as you're not able to come up
with a terrible illness before then." He smiled. "You know," he said,
"most young girls are afraid right before they get married. Your
mother was terrified when we were married."

"Really?"

"Yes. It was also an arranged marriage. She didn't know what I
would be like."

"But you're different, Father," she protested.

"Yes," he said, "I am. But there are other men who are different
too. Portia assures me that the man you are marrying is a good person. He is kind and gentle. Who knows? You may be as happy with
him as your mother was with me."

She smiled. "Don't be silly, Father. There's no one in this world
as good as you are."

He laughed. "That's what all fathers like to hear from their little
girls. But it's not true. There are good men out there, and I believe
you will be happy with Cornelius. But right now I want you to think
about eating and building up your strength. This isn't something
that either of us can change, so we need to get on with it, with grace,
and whatever it takes for you to do that, I suggest you start now."

Antonia sat up. He father leaned over and gave her a hug.

"Pilate has given me some time off to spend with you," he said. "Why don't you have your servants help you get dressed, and, if you're feeling well enough, I'll take you to the bazaar and let you choose some new things to take with you."

"Shopping!" Antonia said, brightening up.

"Yes, we're going shopping."

"I won't be long," she said with new energy.

"I didn't think so. I'll be waiting for you out by the portico."

* * *

Antonia drew in a deep breath and let it out slowly, trying to calm herself. It was over. Cornelius, accompanied by his men of the elite Italian Band, had come from Caesarea for the wedding.

Pilate and Portia had thrown them a wonderful wedding feast befitting a daughter of theirs instead of a houseguest that wouldn't go away.

Cornelius was a handsome man, and he seemed popular with all of his men as well as with his superiors, something Antonia knew was a difficult balance to achieve in the Roman military.

Now she sat on the edge of the bed in the candlelight. The giggling servants had helped her undress and put on her special wedding night garments that Portia had given her. Now she was just waiting for her husband. Her thoughts kept traveling back over the wall to the Temple and the courtyard.

"God of Yeshua," she whispered, "where are You now? Why are You letting this happen to me?" Then she looked down and felt guilty. Worse things had happened to followers of Yeshua. She could hardly complain, being married off to a successful centurion. "I know I sound ungrateful," she whispered in the darkness, "but I just thought You would figure out some way for me to run away from here and become one of Your followers. But I don't even know where Your followers are now. I haven't seen anyone in the Temple courtyard since—well, that day."

Somehow she couldn't even bring herself to talk about the stoning, not even to Yeshua's God. Covering her face with her hands, she shuddered. "I still want to be Your follower, even if I can't be with any of the others. Please help me to do what I need to do in this life with grace and dignity, and please help me to find other followers."

She would have prayed more, but the door opened and her new husband entered the room. "I see you're all ready," he said.

Shyly she looked at the floor.

As he sat down on the bed he seemed like another person in his soft robe instead of the centurion armor and the red-feathered helmet. "I know," he said, "I look different."

In spite of herself she smiled.

For a moment he seemed lost for words, then blurted, "We need to talk. I don't know how to say this, but I must be honest with you." Another pause. "There are things that—that I feel I must tell you, though—he looked away—"I suppose it could wait for later."

A mixture of emotions surged through her—fear, curiosity, confusion. Glancing at him, she said, "T-t-tell me . . . now."

He took a deep breath. It suddenly occurred to Antonia that perhaps her new husband felt as awkward as she did, but why? Whoever heard of centurions being uncomfortable about anything?

"You may not be thrilled to be married to me," he said, "once I have explained this, but I feel that it's only fair for you to know."

What could possibly be bothering Cornelius? Was it something shameful? But, strangely, already she felt protective of him. Reaching out, she touched his shoulder. "But we are married now," she said, "so whatever your secret is, it is my secret too."

He looked at her, and a very small and tentative smile formed around his lips. "I—I've never been much of a worshiper of the gods."

Suddenly Antonia started to chuckle. "Here in Judea being a worshiper of the gods doesn't exactly make you popular."

"That's true," he said, his smile growing a little more, "but I don't intend to live here in Judea all my life."

"My father is planning to move back to Rome someday too."

"Yes," Cornelius said, glancing away. "While I have lived here in Judea I—I have met a lot of . . . interesting people."

She waited for him to continue.

He turned to her. "Have you ever heard of Yeshua of Nazareth?"

Startled, she immediately wondered if her new husband had found out her secret. Was he going to annul the marriage because of her beliefs? Was this the way out that God was providing for her? "Yes," she said, taking a deep breath, "I have." Should she tell him more? Instead she remained silent.

Cornelius looked at the floor. "I've become a believer." He looked at her. "I have not told anyone, although my men realize that something is different. I'm not sure how to be a believer, since I'm not Jewish and don't intend to become a Jew." Then the words began to burst out. "So I have worshiped Him privately, and I pray to Him and have tried to care for the people under my authority with fairness and to do everything the way I believe Yeshua would do it or how He would want me to." He paused for breath.

Suddenly Antonia didn't know whether to laugh or to cry. Cornelius wasn't accusing her of being a believer—he was confessing that *he* was. She flung her arms around his neck.

Startled, he said, "What is it?"

"I'm a believer too," she whispered, now choking up. "I didn't know what to do. I've been watching them from the wall here and knew I could never be one. They won't let me in there. But I've been praying to the God of Yeshua. I've even been praying to Yeshua because I think that He's in heaven, too, according to what I've heard. I was praying that something would happen so that I wouldn't have to get married because I thought you would worship the Roman gods. And here God answered my prayer by marrying me to the only other Roman believer I have ever met—besides Portia." She caught her breath. "Cornelius, you can't tell anybody about Portia. Pilate knows, but . . ."

"I understand. I would never tell a secret that would compromise the safety of the wife of my governor."

Antonia looked into his eyes. "I don't believe you would," she said finally. "Oh, Cornelius, God has given me a husband who's also a believer and probably the only other man in the world I can trust besides my father."

He laughed as he brushed his fingers through her hair. "That's pretty high praise. I mean—fathers are hard competition."

"But I think you'll be fine," she said with a blush.

"I certainly hope so." Laughing, they snuggled in each other's arms.

I laughed too, although thankfully they couldn't hear me since having a third person in the room would have startled the newlyweds. But it filled me with joy to see how the Mighty One had done it again. Apart from being the Creator and the most powerful and intelligent being in the universe, He is also its greatest romantic. And it is a pleasure every day just serving Him.

Elihu Ben Malchus

W ake up, Elihu; you can't sleep all day!"

Elihu felt his aunt's foot gently prodding his ribs. He rolled over and yawned.

"Come on," she said. "The sun is almost up. If you wait too long, everything at the fish market will be picked over, and we'll end up eating the leftovers."

The boy groaned. Life in Capernaum was nothing like the one he was used to. Ever since the night in the garden when Yeshua of Nazareth had been arrested Elihu's father had been sick. One of Yeshua's followers had cut his father's ear off with a sword, and Yeshua had picked it up, looked gently into the eyes of the chief servant of His greatest enemy, and replaced his ear. It had healed perfectly.

The ear had nothing to do with Malchus's illness. His problem was going back to work for the high priest who had engineered the execution of the Nazarene. Sometimes the body has a way of providing an escape through illness when the mind can't figure a way out.

With another yawn Elihu stood up. "It's barely daytime. What is it that you need me to do?"

"I think some fresh fish would be nourishing for your father. Up there in the city you probably live on that nasty dried fish from the market or the salted kind or fish that's been sitting around half the day waiting to get there. We're going to feed your father some real food and get him well again."

"You're right about the fish," Elihu said with a smile. "Many things we get in Jerusalem are very good, but the fish isn't so great."

"Well, fish is what your father needs right now," his aunt insisted. "I want you to go down to the market. The fishermen have been out all night and usually arrive back about this time. You can get the best stuff if you are there when they first return."

Sleepily Elihu nodded.

"You know how to select good fish, don't you?"

The boy laughed. "Yes," he said. "Just because I live in the city doesn't mean that my education has been totally lacking."

She chuckled and ruffled his hair that was already tangled and tousled and standing straight up from his night's sleep. "Fine. Get yourself down to the shore and see what they caught last night."

Elihu would do almost anything to see his father doing better, although he didn't think that food was the real problem. Turning, he walked toward the lakeshore.

He enjoyed watching the fishermen sort the fish. They flung the good fish into the big stone holding tanks built for that purpose by their docks, and the unclean fish and other water creatures got thrown into baskets to be sold to the Gentiles or fed to animals.

As he selected a large beautiful fish from the stone tank he double-checked as always to make sure it had both fins and scales, for no self-respecting Jew would ever consider eating a fish that didn't have both. After all, that was the law!

When he reached into his money pouch for a coin to pay the fisherman he suddenly let out an involuntary shriek and dropped both the fish and the pouch with a splash into one of the tanks. It startled the fisherman, too. All the color had drained from

Elihu's face as he pointed a finger.

"You're—you're that man," he said.

"I—I—I—I don't know what you're talking about," the person stammered.

"That night in the garden—you're the one with the sword. My father's ear . . . "

Although obviously rattled, the fisherman took a deep breath, seemed to calm himself, and drew himself up to his full height. "Yes, my name is Peter, and I was there that night. Is your father well?"

"No," Elihu said sadly, "but his ear is fine."

The fisherman smiled. "Well, the Master fixed that part of him. That will probably be good forever. What is his other trouble?"

"His stomach," the boy said. "He's been unable to eat or keep any food down ever since then. And he hasn't been able to work."

The big man nodded. "I'm sure it's hard for him to serve the high priest after the Master healed his ear."

"I think that's part of the problem," Elihu said after considering a moment.

The big fisherman dug his toe into the dirt as though he was thinking about something difficult. The silence stretched on until it was almost uncomfortable.

"Do you think that your father would allow me to speak to him?" the fisherman asked finally.

"I don't know. Would you be willing to do that?"

"You see," Peter said slowly, "I was very afraid that night. I don't usually go around cutting people's ears off."

They both laughed awkwardly.

"I—I did worse things that night. I also denied I ever knew the Master."

"It was a horrible night and—and it was all a terribly frightening weekend," Elihu said.

"Well," Peter continued, "that's what I was getting to. You see,

I've seen Him since then. He met me here on the beach. He even fixed breakfast for my friends and me. But He forgave me for all that I did. I was able to get over my paralyzing depression and fish again."

"So you know what my father is feeling?"

"Maybe not exactly the same, but yes, some of it."

Elihu smiled. "Well, if you'll help me find my money pouch in this wriggling mess of fish, I'll go home and ask him."

Soon both of them were in the tank up to their armpits and feeling around for the missing pouch.

A week later Elihu was happy to be back in Jerusalem. He didn't know what Peter had said to his father during their secret meeting, but Malchus had been in a better mood ever since and was eager to get back to work, which was good because the Feast of Weeks was quickly approaching. It was the great harvest festival where Jews came from all over the country, and the high priest's office was extremely busy. Annas was delighted to have Malchus back.

"No one else is able to run everything as smoothly," the religious leader told him as he welcomed his servant back.

Malchus thanked him but said very little.

I was happy to be back in Jerusalem too. The risen Son of the Mighty One was making appearances in Jerusalem, and I hated being away from where the action was. Just being where He might show up was exciting.

Peter had returned to Jerusalem too, to meet with the others and discuss what to do next.

I had a great sense of anticipation, and it appeared to be catching. Elihu was on his way home from the Temple after delivering something for his father. Suddenly he did a double take. Could it be? Surely not! The last time he'd seen Peter it was in Capernaum, yet it looked like him. Elihu quickened his steps to catch up. The man ahead of him was in a hurry, moving with long strides. He had pulled his cloak up over his head, so it was difficult to see his face.

Yet Elihu was almost sure. The man turned several corners and dodged into a shop, but the boy stayed right behind him.

Finally Peter spun around. "Why are you following me?" he demanded.

"It is you!" Elihu said.

"Oh," Peter replied, recognizing the boy, "it is me. Why are you following me?"

"I was just happy to see you. My father has done so much better since you spoke with him."

"It wasn't me," the man said softly. "It was the Lord's doing. I'm not all that special."

Elihu grinned. "Well, I'm happy to see you, anyway."

The fisherman smiled, then quickly glanced around. "You mustn't follow me, nor should you be seen with me. It's dangerous. I don't want to get caught, and I don't want to get you in trouble, so please don't follow me."

"Well, I was wondering something," Elihu said, screwing up his courage. "You said that Yeshua met you and fixed you breakfast that day. Is He around?"

Peter again looked over his shoulder. "We've seen Him. He joins us occasionally."

"Here in Jerusalem?"

Peter nodded. "That's why I'm here."

"I want to see Him," the boy declared.

Peter's glance softened. "We're meeting later today—out on Olivet."

Elihu nodded. He knew where the place was on the Mount of Olives.

"You may come, but don't bring anyone with you and don't tell anyone where you're going."

"I won't. Will He be there?"

"I don't know," Peter said slowly.

"Well, I will be," Elihu promised.

"Fine." Peter glanced around once more. "Now stop following me and go do something useful."

"Yes, sir," Elihu said with a grin and turned to walk the other way.

After stopping at home for lunch, Elihu then headed for the Mount of Olives.

It wasn't that far. It was just that it seemed all uphill. Jerusalem itself perched on top of several ridges and deep valleys, and more hills surrounded the city.

The sun beat down on him as he kept trudging. "It's only a Sabbath day's journey," he mumbled to himself. "It's not that far." The cool shade of the olive trees and the fragrance of the garden were welcome after crossing the valley.

The boy looked around. It wasn't long before he came upon a small group not far from where Yeshua of Nazareth had been arrested that horrible night. Although they looked at him suspiciously, he quietly joined them.

Suddenly his heart did a flip-flop. Yeshua stood right in front of them! Elihu stared at the scars on His hands and wrists from the iron spikes that had fastened Him to the cross. It was really Him!

As Yeshua made His way around the group, speaking to everyone, Elihu became terrified as He got closer and closer. Would He recognize him as the son of the servant of the man who had engineered His arrest and unfair trial? Yeshua looked into Elihu's eyes and put His hand on his shoulder. Suddenly Elihu knew everything was going to be fine and that he was going to worship this Man or this God or whoever Yeshua of Nazareth was as long as he lived.

Yeshua sat and spoke with them for a long time. "I'm going to leave you," He said finally. "I want you to stay in Jerusalem until My Spirit comes and joins you. I may not be with you in My body, but I will be with you through the Spirit. And He will lead you and comfort you. But you must stay together here in Jerusalem until that happens."

Everyone in the crowd nodded or murmured their consent.

Then all of a sudden in the middle of His speaking and before anyone realized what was happening, Yeshua started to rise. Elihu caught his breath sharply. No, his eyes weren't deceiving him. Yeshua was getting higher and higher now. Everyone watched in silence and shock as He ascended higher and higher until the glare of the sun blurred their vision and the clouds swallowed Him up.

"He's gone!" someone exclaimed.

Everyone gazed at the sky and then each other, trying to figure out what had just happened. Certainly Yeshua was gone, but where?

Suddenly they noticed that two strangers had joined them. They were dressed all in white without a single proper Jewish blue thread decorating the edge of their garments.

"Why are you staring so?" one of the men asked. "This same Yeshua is going to be back. He'll return exactly the same way as you saw Him go."

Elihu released his breath. He felt as if he'd been holding it for hours. "So He's coming back," he whispered to himself. "Oh, thank You, God!"

Suddenly the men were gone too.

"Where did they go?" someone asked. "They were just here. Maybe they were angels."

The crowd started murmuring.

"I guess none of us really understand what just happened," Peter said, "except that Yeshua has left us. But He did tell us we need to stay in Jerusalem until He returns. Perhaps we can rent that room that we all met in the night before His arrest. That should have enough space for most of us. But for now let's head back into the city and just try to keep everything a secret."

With nods and comments of "Yes, that's a good idea," the little knot of people headed back toward the city in twos and threes.

Elihu just sat under a big olive tree. His mind raced so fast that he could hardly keep up with his thoughts. What would happen now? What would they do once they went back to the city? How could they tell when Yeshua's Spirit came? Would His believers let him join the group?

Suddenly he stood to his feet. *No matter what the others think or decide, I'm a believer. I'm a follower of Yeshua, and I will do what it takes to be there when His Spirit comes in whatever way that is.* He drew himself up to his full height and strode purposefully back down the hill toward the city.

Though Elihu kept his eyes open for any signs of Yeshua's followers, he saw no one. It had been 10 days now, and he was afraid that they had gotten their message and the Spirit of Yeshua had come and then they had left without him.

Why? he wondered. *I prayed to the Almighty One, the Father. And I prayed to Yeshua, His Son. I believe He is God's Son. I asked to be included among His followers. But I haven't heard anything. Perhaps Yeshua just wants me to be a follower later.*

He shrugged. It was so hard to know what to do next. Meanwhile he would just do what his father told him, unless God or Yeshua showed him otherwise.

It was the Festival of Weeks, the first of the wheat harvest— Elihu's favorite festival of the year. Everyone gathered from all over Israel at the Temple. No one would work on that day, just celebrate and relax.

Visitors packed the city. The colonnades and courtyards of the Temple buzzed like a veritable beehive. And his father, who was now looking much healthier, raced around like a chicken with its head cut off, trying to keep up with all of the high priestly duties and events that he coordinated for the high priest.

Excitement definitely hung in the air. And though it was just 10:00 in the morning, the excitement of some people in the crowd seemed to have pushed them a little over the edge. Several jumped up onto the steps and started preaching and shouting.

Elihu shook his head. "There's a few in every crowd," he chuckled to himself. Suddenly he stopped. Could it be? It was the burly fisherman he had met in Capernaum!

When Elihu edged closer, he saw that it looked like Peter, but it certainly didn't sound like him. Preaching loudly and boldly, he no longer seemed afraid. And he was talking about Yeshua.

The youth stopped to listen.

"Hey, Elihu, I haven't seen you in a while," his friend Stephen nudged him.

"Where have you been?" Elihu asked, turning to him.

"Oh, uh—around."

"Well," Elihu said, "we spent a couple weeks with my aunt while my father was so sick, but we're back now."

Stephen pointed to Peter. "He's saying some pretty amazing things."

"Yes. Were you here that week when Yeshua was crucified?"

Stephen nodded. "It was terrible."

After carefully glancing around, Elihu whispered, "He's been back, you know."

Suddenly Stephen also looked around. "I know," he said, his words barely audible. "I saw Him."

"Really? Me too."

"I know. I noticed you up on the hill on Olivet the day He left."

"You were there?"

"Yes. You seemed to be lost in your thoughts at the time."

Elihu sighed. "I was. I had a lot on my mind. But now I'm a believer in Him."

Stephen broke into a huge smile. "Me too."

Their attention turned to Peter and the other preachers.

"I never thought of him as much of a speaker," Elihu commented, indicating Peter.

Stephen laughed. "Me neither. It's the Spirit."

"The Spirit?"

"Uh-huh. There were 120 of us all packed into that little room, waiting and praying. It had been 10 days, and none of us went anywhere because we knew that He would send His Spirit. He had said He would. And suddenly we heard a sound like rushing wind, and then it was like fire. It just swept through the room and filled all of us who were there. And—and it just makes such a difference. The biggest one, I think, is that it took away all of our fear."

"Well, it certainly took his away," Elihu said, gesturing toward Peter.

"Well, think about it. Most of Yeshua's followers are uneducated. Definitely not the ones you would expect to be up here preaching. Yet listen to them. It's Yeshua's Spirit. He's with us." Stephen's voice had a note of awe in it.

Elihu broke into a smile. "As long as He's with us in body or in Spirit, things will be fine."

"Yes, and they will no matter how they may look at times. But you know what really amazes me?"

"What?" Elihu asked.

"How did a fisherman like Peter learn to speak fluent Greek?"

"Greek? I've never heard him speak Greek. A fisherman like him would know only Aramaic."

"Well," Stephen said, "he's speaking in Greek now. That's what I grew up speaking as a little boy. I know Greek when I hear it."

Elihu listened carefully, but Peter was definitely using Aramaic, the language that most local people spoke. Then he shook his head. "I don't hear anyone speaking Greek."

They glanced around. The variety of clothing styles indicated that many pilgrims and visitors from other countries had come to the Temple for the religious festival.

Curious, Elihu began to eavesdrop on what they were saying to each other. "How did he learn to speak my language?" a man with what Elihu thought was an Egyptian accent said to the person next to him.

"He's not speaking your language," replied his companion. "He's speaking Gallic from the northern tribes."

"No, no. I'm from Persia. I recognize my home language when I hear it," insisted a third.

When Elihu looked at Stephen, his friend whispered, "It's a miracle."

"My father used to tell me a story when I was little about a tower called Babel where God confused all the languages and no one could understand each other anymore," Elhu replied after a pause. "Perhaps this is God doing just the opposite so that no matter what language it is that Peter's speaking, everyone hears it in their own tongue."

"Praise God!" Stephen exclaimed, then glanced around in concern to see if anyone had heard him. He lowered his voice. "The miracles just never end. Not only has He provided the speakers with enough courage to preach, but He's made it possible for everyone here to understand it, no matter where they're from."

This is the best Feast of Weeks ever, Elihu thought, grinning to himself.

The rest of the week Elihu spent as much time as he could at the Temple. It was not difficult to come up with reasons, for the Temple was a whirl of activity as the festival celebrations wound down.

A few days later Elihu saw Stephen in the courtyard again. He was careful not to draw attention to himself as he edged over near the young Greek-speaking Jew. "Stephen, the other day I went around the courtyard eavesdropping and asking people where they had come from."

"And what did you find out?"

"Well, apparently Peter wasn't just speaking in Greek and Aramaic. I counted at least 15 different language groups of people who claimed he was preaching in their dialect. Places such as Libya and Egypt and Cappadocia, even as far away as Mesopotamia and Cyrene. Everywhere."

Stephen chuckled. "I'm not surprised. If we were hearing it in our languages, it shouldn't be hard to believe they did in theirs. And you know what I learned? The word among the believers is that we now number about 3,000 here in Jerusalem, instead of just 120."

Elihu shook his head as a thought struck him. "Now those 3,000 will all go home from the festival. Then there will be groups of believers sprouting up everywhere."

"Everywhere Jews live," Stephen added.

"And soon everyone everywhere will have heard of—well, you know who."

Stephen was about to say something else when a great clamor from the gate caught their attention.

"Wonder what's going on," Elihu said. "Let's go see."

The two hurried over. In the midst of a group of people stood Peter and John and the beggar who had been lying on his pallet next to the gate begging alms from everyone who came in. He was doing some ecstatic little dance that required a lot more agility than anyone in his physical condition should have been able to muster.

"What happened to him?" asked Elihu.

"I've been healed! I've been healed!" the beggar shouted to everyone. "When I asked these two men for money, they said that they didn't have any but that they would give me what they did have. Then they healed me in the name of Yeshua of Nazareth."

The two friends' eyes met. While neither of them had been brave enough to speak the name inside the Temple walls, the beggar had no such hesitance.

"Isn't it wonderful! I've been lame so long. This is marvelous! I must show the priests that I've been healed; then I must find my family." He broke into joyful laughter.

Peter and John stepped up onto the low platform the beggar had been lying on. It was the perfect opportunity to speak to the growing crowd.

Elihu shook his head. "They must be brave to heal in Yeshua's name with the priests and Temple guards all around," he whispered.

"Yes," his friend said quietly. "I feel guilty that I'm not that brave. But I have a young wife and two children to take care of. I just don't have the courage."

"I understand. I don't either. My father would really be upset."

"Despite his stomach ailment going away after a visit from the fisherman?"

"I don't know. We've not discussed it."

"Maybe you should," Stephen suggested.

"Maybe so."

Peter and John continued to preach, and the crowd grew larger and larger. Elihu could see the priests on duty back on the marble steps pacing back and forth and getting more and more agitated.

"I feel trouble brewing," Elihu muttered.

Sure enough, a group of the priests on duty, the captain of the Temple guard, and some Sadducees who were always involved in everything that went on rushed over, grabbed the two followers of Yeshua, and dragged them off.

The crowd slowly dispersed, the people mumbling quietly to themselves.

"What do you think they'll do with them?" Stephen asked.

"Probably turn them over to the Romans. They'll be put in the dungeons in the Antonia Fortress next to the Temple here until they can have a trial."

"Do you think they'll crucify them, too?" Stephen said, concern in his voice.

Elihu was quiet for a moment. "I don't think so. The Jewish leaders have not gotten over all of the problems caused by the previous crucifixion. I think they'll try to settle it more quietly if they can."

"I hope so. Let me know if you find out anything."

"Oh, I can find out plenty," Elihu replied. "It's just that I can't do anything about it."

Stephen slowly smiled. "I guess the Lord has each of us in a spot where He wants us right now. And when He wants you to do something, He'll let you know and make a way."

"Yes, I suppose so. But will I have the courage to do it when that time comes?"

"I guess none of us know that until then," Stephen said with a shrug. "But if His Spirit can make bold preachers out of those two fishermen, I guess He can do almost anything."

That evening Elihu climbed the steps to the flat roof of his home. His father sat there enjoying the cool night air.

"Father—" the boy began.

"What, son?"

"May I talk to you?"

"Of course. You can always talk to me, Elihu."

"Well, i—i—it's about something important and—well, I don't want to get anybody in trouble."

Malchus sighed. "There are a lot of things like that these days, aren't there?"

Elihu sat down by his father.

Malchus lowered his voice. "I want you to know, my son, that no matter what it is, you can talk to me, and even if we disagree strongly, I will not betray your secrets. You are my son, and I love you more than anything else."

"I'm really glad," the boy said hesitantly, "because—I—I've—I've been—"

"I know what you've been doing," his father interrupted. "I've been watching you."

"You have?" Elihu said in surprise.

"Of course. These are dangerous times. A lot is going on in Jerusalem, and I'm concerned for your safety."

Elihu sat silently for a bit, then said timidly, "I've become a believer."

"Ah," said his father, staring into the distance. "That would explain why you keep talking to them."

"Well, yes. I didn't know you knew."

"It's my job to know such things. Remember whom I am servant to?"

They sat in silence again.

"Please be careful," his father said finally. "The Temple guards arrested Peter and John today."

"Yes, I was there. Do you think that they'll be crucified, as He was?"

His father shook his head. "I sincerely doubt it at this point. No one's gotten over what happened at Passover yet. My guess is that they'll probably give them a stiff warning and see if they can't intimidate them into not preaching anymore. Besides," he added, "rumor has it that there are up to 5,000 believers now. Many of them are still in Jerusalem, and I think the priests are afraid of making them angry."

"Father, do—do you believe Yeshua of Nazareth was the Messiah?"

Malchus lowered his gaze and thought before he spoke. "I don't know, son. The uncertainty—I think it was what was making me ill."

"But you're better now. Did you decide something?"

Malchus shook his head. "It was what the fisherman said to me."

"Peter?"

"Yes."

"What did he say, Father?"

"Peter reminded me that the night that he cut my ear off Yeshua restored it without hostility. That His look was kind, as if He forgave me for being part of the group. The fisherman told me that He forgave me then and that He forgave me now, and that forgiveness was not based on whether or not I had made my choice. I still need to make a choice, but knowing that I was forgiven took away all the pain in my stomach. I just don't see how I can work for the high priest who plotted His death and who is busy trying to erase the memory of His ever being here when He was such a good man."

"As long as you believe only that He was a good man, you can still work for the high priest," Elihu said. "But if you really believe He was the Messiah, it will make it hard."

Malchus sighed. "It is hard," he agreed.

Elihu hugged him. "I love you, Father."

"I love you too. Somehow we'll figure this out together."

Malchus was right about what would happen to Peter and John. The next day after warning and threatening the men, the Temple authorities set them free. It was not long before they were back in the Temple talking to the people as they had been before.

In the following days Elihu found himself looking forward to going to the Temple each morning. The errands and tasks assigned him as the son of the high priest's servant took him around the courtyard of women where the Yeshua believers met every day. Able to listen to most of what was going on, he got to know who the believers were. They greeted him each day as they came and went.

Not everyone was happy about the believers meeting in the Temple courts, though there wasn't much they could do about it. Saul, one of the younger but well-respected Pharisees, stopped Elihu one morning.

"Young man," he said, "I've been watching you since you were a child. You are a good son of Israel. Just keep in mind what the Scriptures say, and you'll be all right."

The boy must have looked puzzled, so Saul continued, "You know the psalm 'Blessed is the man that walketh not in the counsel of the ungodly, nor standeth in the way of sinners, nor sitteth in the seat of the scornful'?"

Slowly Elihu nodded. "Yes, sir. I will keep the psalm in mind."

Saul stared hard at him for several moments, then said, "Good. Carry on." And turning on his heel, he walked back toward the gate.

The young man shook his head. *I sure wouldn't want him for an enemy,* he thought.

But all thought of Saul soon left his mind as he drifted back toward the group of believers. It fascinated him how they took care of each other. Anyone who came in with a need soon had it filled by another believer, and not just with a handout. Often the other believers provided ways to earn money or the funds to purchase the tools to start their own craft or to continue what they had been taught before. It was as if everyone belonged to a large family.

One day Joseph came in carrying a heavy satchel. He walked straight up to Peter and dropped it at his feet. Then, untying it, he dumped the contents out. It was filled with coins. Everyone caught their breath.

"I sold a field," he said in his accented Aramaic, for Joseph was from the island of Cyprus. "And I brought the money to you to use however you need it."

Everyone was delighted.

"That is great!" Peter said. "We do need some more money for food for the widows. God bless you. I think we should call you Barnabas, son of encouragement, instead of Joseph."

"Yes, Barnabas is a good name for him," someone agreed.

The name spread through the crowd, and pretty soon everyone was echoing it. The believers never called him Joseph again.

"Look at that," one woman said to her husband.

Elihu glanced over at her. She was beautiful. He edged a little closer to the couple. Eavesdropping on people at the Temple was one of his favorite pastimes.

"Everybody is going to respect him from now on," the woman continued. "What an easy way to become looked up to by the whole community."

Her husband made some noncommittal grunt.

"No, I'm serious," she said. "We should try that. Wouldn't it be nice to have people honor us that way?"

Elihu's forehead creased into a frown. *H'mm,* he thought, *I thought that people liked and respected Barnabas because he's a really nice man and he happened to give the money because he was a good man and not the other way around.* But he said nothing.

A few days later he saw the woman's husband approaching the knot of believers in the corner of the courtyard. He was carrying a heavy bag much like the one Barnabas of Cyprus had brought a few days before. Just as Barnabas had, he set it down in front of Peter.

"What have you got, my friend?" the fisherman asked.

"My name is Ananias," he said. "My wife and I decided to sell a plot of land and give all the proceeds to the group, just as Barnabas did."

"May God bless you. That's wonderful!"

Suddenly a frown crossed Peter's face. "Is this the amount you pledged? The full amount you got for the land?"

"Oh, absolutely," Ananias laughed, "and you're welcome to it. Every penny."

Peter frowned more. "Why are you doing this, Ananias? The land was yours. God didn't say that you had to sell it. When you did, the money was yours. Again, God didn't say that you had to give it all. But you promised to give it all and you swear here publicly that you have. And yet the Holy Spirit knows that you kept back part of it on purpose. Why do you lie to us and lie to the Holy Spirit? You didn't have to lie. You could have given any part of it you wanted to. Did you think that God wouldn't know?"

Ananias clutched his hands to his chest. He shook his head and looked as if he were about to say something, then turned a gray color and collapsed to the ground.

Shrieks of dismay spread through the crowd. Somebody leaped forward and felt Ananias's neck for a pulse. "He's dead," the man said, rising to his feet.

"Dead? He's dead?" people repeated.

"Take him away," Peter commanded.

Some young men wrapped him up and carried him away for burial. A somber crowd clustered around Peter as he tried to comfort them and explain to them that God had not struck him dead because he had kept part of the money. That Ananias had died for lying to God and the rest of the church.

Some time later the beautiful woman whom Elihu had seen with Ananias before now approached the group of believers. She wore a striking sapphire-colored gown and had a gold band to hold her hair in place. The crowd spread and let her through as she approached Peter.

"May I help you?" he asked.

"Yes," she said. "I'm Sapphira—Ananias's wife. He came here a little while ago with our gift, but he hasn't returned home."

"Yes," said Peter. "I have the gift here."

She smiled radiantly.

"Is this the whole amount that you and your husband pledged?"

"Oh, absolutely."

Peter looked into her eyes.

"Yes," she said, suddenly nervous. "We pledged that whatever we got for that piece of land we would give to the community of believers and, well—this is it."

"Is this the whole amount?" Peter asked again.

"Of course! Did you count it? Isn't it enough?"

"So you are in on this too. The plan to lie to us and to the Holy Spirit? Did you think you could lie to God and He wouldn't mind?"

"We—we—how did you know?"

"The young men who carried your husband away are just re-turning," Peter said. "And they will carry you away too."

"I don't know what you're talking about," she snapped, then pressed her hand against her chest. With a faint "Oh" she fell to the stone pavement of the Temple colonnade.

The men picked her up to bury with her husband.

Elihu started shaking and couldn't stop. Being a believer was a wonderful thing, but it could be scary sometimes. Then he shook his head as he realized that God had always been able to read the human heart. "At least I've always known that," he mumbled to himself. Still, what had just happened created a strong feeling of awe. God was to be worshiped and admired and treated with great respect. With a shudder he returned to his duties. Sometimes it felt really good just to work hard and not think about things.

Sulimon

ulimon yawned quietly as sweat trickled down his face. The occasional stray breeze lurking in the Gaza desert brought only another blast of heat. Today, though, the air was absolutely still and stifling. The lord treasurer was totally oblivious to his young servant as he read haltingly out loud from the scroll he had purchased in Jerusalem.

This part of the trip might be long and hot and boring, but it was the most exciting month Sulimon had ever had in his life. The lord treasurer had traveled clear to Jerusalem to worship the God Jehovah. It took them 30 days of continuous travel from their home in Ethiopia to reach the city. He shook his head. *How lucky the Jews who live in Israel are,* he thought to himself. *They can assemble together and worship God at all of the feasts, whereas I and the lord treasurer have made the trip of a lifetime. Well, the lord treasurer's lifetime, anyway.* Secretly Sulimon hoped that he would make it back to Israel someday. After all, he was still young, only 15.

The sights and sounds of the holy city, and especially the Temple, had fascinated the young man and stimulated his curiosity.

I had eagerly recorded the questions he had asked and the enthusiasm with which he had worshiped the Mighty One. Now my wingtips quivered as I anticipated the excitement he would feel for what would happen next. The Holy One's Spirit was on the Gaza road with us, and I could not wait to see what His plans were.

When Sulimon glanced behind him he noticed a man running along the road to catch up with them. He wasn't sure whether to mention the man's presence, interrupting the lord treasurer's reading, or not. However, as the man drew nearer, the stranger shouted, "Hello!"

The lord treasurer put his scroll down. "Halt the caravan," he ordered. "Someone is trying to catch up with us."

His chariot stopped, as well the rest of his retinue. They had not been moving very fast, for though he had beautiful horses to draw his elegant chariot, their supplies rode on slow and cantankerous donkeys who were built for strength, not speed.

Sulimon grinned to himself. He was certain that the donkeys were as glad for a break as he was.

The man soon caught up with them, pausing to catch his breath.

Jumping to the ground from the chariot, Sulimon approached the stranger. "Do you wish to speak to the lord treasurer, loyal servant of the Candace, queen mother of Ethiopia?"

The lord treasurer bowed his head slightly behind the boy.

"I am Philip," the man said, "from Jerusalem."

"Ah," the lord treasurer replied. "Philip, a lover of horses?"

The man laughed. "Yes, that is what my name means, although perhaps it should be just one who would love to have horses."

"Your name and your speech," began the lord treasurer. "You don't sound like someone from Jerusalem. You are Greek, yes?"

Philip bowed. "I am."

"Ah, that is good. At least those of us who can speak Greek can communicate, no? After all, Greek is the language of trade and money."

"It is."

Sulimon shifted his weight from one foot to the other. He was dying to know what the man wanted. But the rules of hospitality made the banter mandatory before they could get down to the real purpose of the conversation.

Fortunately, Philip must have been in a hurry, or else he had run out of small talk. "I heard you reading," he said.

The lord treasurer looked up. "Yes, the writings of the prophet Isaiah."

"And you are having trouble understanding them?"

The treasurer laughed. "Of course. I have no one here to explain them to me."

The man broke into a wide grin. So did Sulimon. Suddenly he knew what the man wanted.

"Do you understand them?" asked the lord treasurer.

"I will study them with you," Philip said.

Now it was the treasurer's turn to grin. "Climb in. Ride with me in my chariot. It is a long road. We have plenty of time."

"I would be delighted to."

He stepped up on the chariot. The treasurer signaled, and the caravan resumed its slow progress across the desert.

"Read to me the part you were just at," Philip said.

"'And like a sheep he opened not his mouth,'" began the lord treasurer. When he finished, he turned to Philip. "Whom is the prophet talking about? Himself or someone else?"

"How long were you in Jerusalem?" Philip asked, seeming to ignore the treasurer's question.

"We stayed a little more than a month," the official answered, puzzled. He looked thoughtful. "Many strange things happened while we were there. I heard people constantly discussing a man named Yeshua of Nazareth. His followers seemed to be everywhere even though he had apparently been executed. It was very confusing to us because some of the people we spoke to talked as if he were still alive. Others said he was gone, and some insisted he was dead. Do you know anything about him?"

"I am a follower of His. And Isaiah was speaking of Him."

"This passage seems to be referring to sacrifices. And what does it mean when it speaks about a man of sorrows?"

"Yeshua of Nazareth was a man of sorrows," Philip explained. "The whole sacrificial system was God's way of telling us about Him and pointing to His life when He would send His Son to die for our sins. His life and His blood would pay the penalty for us, so that we would not have to die for our own sins. For thousands of years we have waited for this to happen, but when He came we didn't recognize who He was."

"Oh, it says that here, too," the lord treasurer exclaimed, unrolling part of the scroll. "Here it is. Because he wouldn't be impressive, people wouldn't recognize who he was."

Philip nodded. "And that is what happened. Even though we didn't give Him the honor that He deserved as the Son of Jehovah, He continued through with the plan and offered His life as the Lamb to repair our broken relationship with God."

The treasurer thought a moment. "So it does make sense. I knew it would. The writings of such a great prophet had to have deeper meaning. My people have known of this prophet for hundreds of years."

"They have?" It was Philip's turn to sound surprised.

"Oh, yes. Tell him, Sulimon."

The boy, who had been wanting a chance to join the conversation, flashed a grateful smile at the lord treasurer. "We worship the God of Abraham too."

"You do?" Philip stared at the two men sharing the chariot with him. Their dark skin glistened in the hot sunlight. "But—but you're from Ethiopia," he protested. "What do the Ethiopians know of Abraham and his God?"

The treasurer laughed, taking no offense at Philip's shock. "Do you remember a king you had here in Israel named Solomon?" he asked.

"Well, of course. Solomon was the greatest king ever. Well, maybe David was, but certainly Solomon was the wisest man ever."

The lord treasurer nodded. "Well, young Sulimon here is named for him. There are many of us in my country who worship God Jehovah and keep the holy Sabbath. My young servant Sulimon and I are both worshipers of Jehovah, and we came to Jerusalem to offer sacrifices at the Temple."

"I see." Philip did not know quite what to say. "How did you know of the prophet Isaiah?"

"One of my ancestors," Sulimon said, "was Ebed-melech. Have you heard of him?"

Philip paused for a moment. "The name is familiar . . ."

"He was a friend of the prophet Jeremiah," the lord treasurer explained. "When one of your kings imprisoned Jeremiah into a cistern just before Judah went into captivity, Ebed-melech helped pull Jeremiah from it. The prophet especially appreciated the fact that Ebed-melech threw rags down into the pit for Jeremiah to put under his arms so that the ropes wouldn't injure him. Others took the prophet to Egypt for his own safety. And Ebed-melech came south after that to dwell in the country of the Nubians. Many of his descendants still live among my people. I had heard many stories of the prophets Isaiah and Jeremiah, and, while in Jerusalem on our trip, I bought this scroll so that we could read some of the great prophetic writings for ourselves."

Philip laughed. "Imagine our God coordinating events so that we could meet here today and study the scroll together."

They continued to study and talk, a few verses at a time, exclaiming again and again about God's goodness and how the prophecies suddenly made sense when seen from the perspective of Yeshua's life.

It seemed as if they had been talking for only a short time, yet by now the sun hung low over the horizon as they rounded a bend in the road and came across a small body of water.

The lord treasurer grabbed Philip's arm. "Is there anything to prevent me from being baptized here?" he asked. They had been talking for some time not only about the prophecies of Isaiah, but about the growth of the group of believers.

"Nothing. Surely the Lord would not coordinate everything as He has to give us this time to study and come to this water if He did not intend for you to be baptized and become one of His."

"Would you baptize me, too?" Sulimon asked as they stepped down from the chariot and started toward the little pond.

"Of course," Philip smiled.

"Does this make me fully one of the group of believers?" asked the Ethiopian. He looked down at the ground. "As a eunuch I was not allowed into the Temple."

Philip shook his head sadly. "The body of Christ recognizes no boundaries even though our people used to do so. I just came back from preaching in Samaria. It wasn't that long ago that the disciples, those closest to Yeshua Himself, hated the Samaritans. In fact, John even asked Yeshua once to pour down fire and burn up a city in Samaria. But on my last trip there I baptized many people. And Peter and John came up there into Samaria and laid hands on them, and the Holy Spirit filled the Samaritan believers.

"As a believer in the body of Christ we are equal." He touched the Ethiopian's shoulder. "We draw no lines between Jews, Greeks, men, women, eunuchs, rich, poor. We are all one. He died for all of us."

They waded into the water. "Sulimon and I will take everything you have taught us to the court of the queen mother," the lord treasurer announced. "In fact, I will make young Sulimon my spokesperson, for I stay very busy in the treasury. But I will give him my authority, and he can teach what you have explained to us. Many will be delighted to hear and will want to become Yeshua's followers."

"And you will be the Lord Yeshua's first missionaries to your country," Philip said. "I am honored to have met you and been able to share Yeshua with you."

The baptism was quick. As Sulimon stepped out of the water, he turned to Philip to thank him, but the man was no longer there.

"Where did he go?" he asked the lord treasurer.

Surprised, the lord treasurer looked around.

"Could he have been an angel?"

"I don't think so," his master replied. "He said that he was a man—that he was a follower of Yeshua. I believe he was, but perhaps the Spirit of Yeshua swept him away to someone else who needed to hear from him, just as we did. After all, he did say that Yeshua's Spirit was here on earth now that Yeshua had gone back to heaven."

Suddenly Sulimon and the lord treasurer broke into joyful laughter. "It doesn't matter," they said in unison.

"Meanwhile, we have much to tell. I can't wait till we get home," Sulimon said. "How good is the God Jehovah and how good His Son, Yeshua, to send His Spirit."

I nodded. They were right about that. Jehovah and His Son, Yeshua, are good. And I am greatly honored to be working for them.

✝HADDEUS

haddeus entered the courtyard with a gigantic bundle of reeds balanced on his head. He walked over to where his father was working, and then paraded back and forth. "Such poise, such balance, such a *large* bundle of reeds. Are you lucky to have me for a son, or what?"

The boy's father looked up and chuckled. "And so brave," he said, "facing all those dangers down there collecting reeds by the river."

"Yes," Thaddeus said, being careful not to nod and drop his bundle. "Fearlessly harvesting reeds, caring not for the roars of the hippos or the crocodiles smiling at me from under the water."

"Yes, but I've heard the real danger was snakes that get into your bundle and slither down to whisper in your ear as you're walking home." He reached over and tickled Thaddeus's ear from behind with a long blade of grass.

With a shriek the boy dropped his bundle and scratched his ear.

"You can scream almost as well as a girl," his father said with a laugh.

"That was a terrible thing to do," his son shouted. "Sometimes I think you're the best father in the world, and other times I think you have a rotten streak running through you. But," he winked at his father, "I'm always so glad to have you back."

His father put his arm around him. "I'm glad to be back too—so glad."

Watching them from above, I nodded. Life was certainly a lot different for this little family since the Mighty Son had healed Thaddeus's father of his demon possession. A few years before, Thaddeus and his mother had struggled in poverty, continually facing the possibility of starvation, while his father ran screaming through the cemeteries, demon-possessed and unaware of his own surroundings most of the time. Now they were a real family.

"I love that we're now a whole family," the boy blurted.

"Well, son," his father said, smiling, "we're going to be even more of a family yet."

"What do you mean?" Thaddeus asked, his brow crinkling.

"You know—mother, father, brothers, sisters."

"Brothers? Sisters?" the boy echoed.

"Yes," his father said happily, "your mother's going to have a baby, and you'll have a brother or a sister."

Thaddeus frowned.

"What's the matter?"

"You and Mother?" Thaddeus mumbled.

"Yes, that's what normal families do. They grow."

The boy shuddered.

"You know about family stuff," his father continued. "We've talked about that."

"Yeah, I know. Other families. But you and Mother?"

His father laughed again. "Yes, Mother and I, just like other families. It will be several months yet, so you have time to get used to the idea and be properly grateful to the Most High when the child actually arrives."

The boy nodded slowly, then shook his head.

I was glad that the humans couldn't hear me when I laughed. Human children always seemed so shocked that their own parents would have normal feelings and create children just as everyone else does. And Thaddeus was no exception.

"Where is Mother right now?" he asked.

"She's over sweeping the other courtyard."

The boy picked up the scattered bundle of reeds from the ground. He had never seen a house with two courtyards before they had moved to Damascus. In Gadara he and his mother had lived in a tiny shack, but many of the more well-to-do pig farmers had homes with courtyards and small rooms built around them.

Uncle Judas' house had been like that at one time, and then he had constructed a second courtyard for his inn. The main inn on the road entering Damascus, it had a large courtyard with a sheltering roof along one wall, supported by wooden posts. The shelter had two rooms at the very end in case the inn had especially wealthy guests who wanted privacy.

The guests who used the shelter received a safe place for them and their animals to sleep overnight. It was enclosed so the animals wouldn't run away, and locked securely at the gate so that no one in Damascus would rob them.

Back in Gadara, Thaddeus and his family had attracted a lot of attention after Yeshua had healed his father. At first everyone was amazed to find him clothed and in his right mind and wanting to continue his life where it had left off before the creeping madness had set in. But the popularity was fleeting. For when Yeshua had cast the spirits out of his father, they had entered a herd of swine up on the hillside. The pigs then ran off a cliff into the Sea of Galilee. Perhaps the demons had stampeded the herd to turn the people against Yeshua. If nothing else, having had the town's economy decimated in a single blow made the local people much less pleased about the healing of Thaddeus's father. Quite frankly the pigs were more valuable to them, and they became angry.

As a result, Thaddeus and his family had to leave. Uncle Judas had invited them to come to his home in Syria. He had offered them a place to stay for as long as they needed at his inn on Straight Street in exchange for their help with the business.

Uncle Judas' wife had recently died, and he had had only daughters. The last one had been married off some years ago, so he had plenty of room and plenty of money, but needed some family and a little help.

It was good for all of them and was working out well. Thaddeus was making new friends and learning some interesting things about Damascus. According to local legend, the city was built on the site where Cain had murdered his brother Abel. When Thaddeus asked how they had kept the site marked even during the Great Flood, everyone just laughed at him and said he would have to ask Noah. Still it was definitely the spot.

Tradition also said that Uz, the grandson of Shem, had built Damascus. And somewhere around here in the land of Uz was where Job had lived. Thaddeus had heard the stories of Job from the rabbi in the synagogue. Even though Damascus was in Syria, it had 30 synagogues in town to accommodate the large Hebrew population. Some Jews had always lived in Damascus—now a lot more did.

Also followers of Yeshua had reached Damascus before Thaddeus and his family ever got there. Especially since the death of the young deacon Stephen in Jerusalem, the followers of Yeshua had fled the holy city in every direction because of the fierce persecution.

The ringleader seemed to be a man people had named Saul the Saint Slayer or, in Jerusalem, just referred to as Saul the Slayer. He spearheaded the campaign to ferret out the followers of Yeshua by learning their secrets, finding their hiding places, and then dragging them out and executing them, whether they were men, women, or children.

Thaddeus took a deep breath. They were lucky that Uncle Judas lived in Syria. What if their only relatives had lived in Jerusalem? He shuddered. Things were probably worse for followers of Yeshua in Jerusalem than they had been for those in Gadara.

He piled the reeds over in the corner where they kept them to dry. *We are greatly blessed,* he thought to himself. *Not just to live with Uncle Judas, but also that Mother grew up in a family of basket weavers, and here in Damascus there are two rivers with plenty of reeds growing free for anybody who wants them.* His family had been able to start a business, and Mother had taught both Thaddeus and his father how to weave baskets. This way, though Uncle Judas was providing them a place to live, they were able to earn their own income and buy the things the family needed.

The boy drew another deep breath. Yes, life was good!

The clamor at the gate announced the presence of guests.

"I need to speak to the innkeeper," a deep voice shouted from outside.

"My name is Judas. I am the keeper of this establishment," the boy's uncle replied as he opened the gate to reveal a tall man standing there. "How may I help you?"

"We had a—a—a problem on the way to Damascus," the man said, "and we need shelter and some help for this man for a few days." He gestured toward someone sitting hunched over on the back of a horse. "Our leader will need someone to help him with personal care while some of us go back to the Sanhedrin and find out what they want to be done now."

"I see," said Uncle Judas. "Who is your leader?"

"His name is Saul."

Uncle Judas stared. So did Thaddeus. "Saul of Tarsus—Saul the Slayer?" Uncle Judas stuttered.

The name of Saul struck fear into hearts of the followers of Yeshua everywhere. Yet the man on the back of the horse hardly looked fearful himself. He seemed much smaller than one would have imagined him. His shoulders drooped, and he had his head-piece wrapped around his face so no one could see it. But he was obviously either quite ill or extremely distraught.

"Bring him in," Uncle Judas said after a long pause. "This young man is Thaddeus, and he will care for Saul's needs as long as he stays here. There will be an extra charge, of course, for the personal care, as well as a surcharge for putting him in a room—for I take it you don't want him out in the courtyard alone."

"We will pay whatever you require," the man answered. "Put him in your best room."

"Ah, very good," said Uncle Judas. "Bring him this way. Can he speak?"

The tall man nodded.

"Very well; place him in here. Thaddeus, you get anything the man asks you for." Then he spoke both to Saul and the other men. "Thaddeus is very shy and doesn't speak much." He stared hard at Thaddeus, as if to say For this week, at least, please be shy and don't talk. "But he will get whatever you need."

Thaddeus understood. He helped the men lift Saul from the back of the horse and assist him onto a pallet in the corner of the room, where he curled up in a fetal position and pulled his prayer shawl up over his face. He certainly did not look very frightening—frightened was more like it.

As if reading his mind, the tall man turned to Thaddeus and said, "He is a very powerful man. He's just ill. The Sanhedrin sent him here after he dealt with the followers of Yeshua in Jerusalem. Rumor has it that Matthew, one of the twelve, has fled here, as well as many other followers."

Thaddeus paled. How could they know about Matthew? Everyone had been extremely careful to keep it a secret.

"I will bring him some water," the boy said. "And some food from the kitchens. Perhaps that will refresh him from his difficult trip."

When he returned, the other men in the group had left, and only the tall one with the deep voice remained.

"I wanted to make sure you got back before I left," he said.

"You're leaving too? No one is going to stay here with—with Saul?"

"It's a bit awkward," the man explained. "I will tell you a little of what happened just so you can understand our position. We came here with Saul with the intent of cleaning the followers of Yeshua out of Damascus. However, something happened along the road."

"An accident?"

"No, not exactly. There was a very bright light and a sound like thunder, although there wasn't a cloud in the sky. The light was so bright that it knocked us to the ground and Saul from his horse."

"He was hurt in the fall?"

"No! Let me finish!" the man said impatiently. "For a shy child who doesn't talk much, you certainly interrupt."

Thaddeus bowed his head and bit his tongue.

"We heard only loud rumbling like thunder, but Saul said that he saw Yeshua Himself. And that Yeshua asked him why he was persecuting Him. The light has stricken Saul blind, though the rest of us were able to see once it subsided. He feels that Yeshua has punished him.

"All this time he thought that the deacon Stephen had committed blasphemy by claiming that he had seen Yeshua at the right hand of God, and yet now Saul claims to have seen Him too. He doesn't know what to do. Now that he is blind he feels he will no longer be of use to the Sanhedrin. And if he tells his story, they may want him killed. Yet if he doesn't share it, he fears something worse might happen to him. He's very ill and confused and depressed." The man shook his head in puzzlement and frustration.

"And the rest of us are just afraid and don't know what to do. I'm going to stay in Damascus, but in a different part of the city.

And I will be back to visit, but not unless I know it's safe. If the Sanhedrin decide to come after him, you will be safe. You just work at the inn, and Saul's just your guest. But treat him well, for he has been an important man. Indeed, he's a leading Pharisee and a student of Gamaliel."

"I will take good care of him," Thaddeus said cautiously.

"Thank you. And I must be going." He put his hand on the smaller man's shoulder. "I'm leaving now, Saul. I will be back in a few days."

Saul did not move or say anything. With a shrug the tall man left.

"Is there anything I can get for you, sir?" Thaddeus asked.

Silence.

"I'm going back to the kitchens for a few minutes, but I will return. Don't worry. We will take good care of you, and everything will be all right."

"No," said the voice under the prayer shawl. "Nothing will ever be all right again."

* * *

"Honest, Father, it is! It's Saul of Tarsus—Saul the Saint Slayer. Right over there, in the other courtyard in one of the rooms."

"Really?" his father said. "He must have run out of followers of Yeshua to kill in Jerusalem."

"Yes, that's what his companion told us. That Saul has official papers from the authorities to extradite fugitive believers."

"I guess that would be us."

"Well, he doesn't look as if he could hurt us very badly," Thaddeus commented.

"That's because he's sick now." His father sighed. "He has quite a reputation for cruelty."

"The tall man said that he is a very important Pharisee. What exactly is a Pharisee?"

Father took a deep breath. "A Pharisee is a very educated Jew who's studied the traditions of the elders as well as the law of Moses. Their interpretations are different from some of those of the Sadducees."

"What kinds of interpretations?"

"Oh, I don't know. I'm not very educated in that stuff. But I know that the Pharisees think that the dead will be resurrected and the Sadducees don't. And the Pharisees believe in angels and the Sadducees don't. Beyond that, I'm not quite sure, but I bet if you asked our guest when he feels better, he could spend days explaining it to you."

"Right now he's just curled up with his prayer shawl pulled over his face so that no one can see him."

"Don't let his looks deceive you," Father said quietly. "What I've heard about him is pretty frightening. He may just be acting ill so that we will feel sorry for him and lower our guard until he finds out where everyone's hiding. Then he'll catch all of us. Don't feel sorry for him, no matter how pitiful he acts. And whatever you do, be very careful of what you say."

"I will, Father."

"And remember, son, it's never just your life that you protect or endanger. It's also my life and the lives of your mother and our coming baby."

"I'll be careful. You can trust me."

"Come here, Thaddeus," Mother called. "Please try to feed some of this stew to our guest. He hasn't had any food or drink for some time now. While I'm not fond of the man, I certainly don't want him to die here with us."

"Maybe he doesn't need food and water," the boy mumbled. "Maybe he just lives on anger."

He hadn't meant for his mother to hear, but she sighed. "Some people seem to," she said. "Still, see what you can do."

Thaddeus took the tray.

The little man shook his head when the boy offered the food.

"It's been three days," Thaddeus said. "You haven't had any food or any water. If you don't drink or eat, you will die."

"That's the general idea, isn't it?" Saul replied. He raised up on one elbow. "I'm being punished. Go away and leave me alone!"

The boy shrugged. "Well, I know you can't see," he said, "but don't you think that if God wanted you to die, He would have just killed you then?"

"You don't understand. I saw Yeshua, the risen Lord in all His glory. How could you understand?"

"I saw Him in His undergarments," Thaddeus blurted without thinking.

"In His undergarments! Blasphemy!" The blind man swung with his fists. "How can you say such things about the Messiah? You blasphemous youth. You should be beaten within an inch of your life."

One of his fists connected with the tray, and it went splattering against the wall, lentils running down the doorpost like teardrops. With his other hand he grabbed Thaddeus by the leg and knocked him to the floor and began flailing his fists wildly against him.

Suddenly a grip as strong as iron seized Saul's wrist. "Not here," he said. "Not my son, and not in my home. You're not at the Sanhedrin now."

The angry little man stiffened.

"If you're going to convince him of anything, you're going to have to do it by persuasion, not violence," Thaddeus's father continued. "You have no jurisdiction here. This is Damascus, remember?"

"That's not true," the angry little Pharisee insisted. "I have official papers right here in my pouch." He felt around for it. "I have the authority of Rome for extradition of fugitive Jewish believers right here in Damascus." His voice trailed off into silence as he realized he no longer had a pouch.

"I expect that your traveling companions have made off with it and whatever money you had."

Saul pulled his prayer shawl over his head again. "Go away," he said distantly.

"Certainly. Come on, Thaddeus."

As they walked out into the courtyard, Thaddeus's father looked at his son's face and said, "You'll have quite a bruise where he hit you."

The boy smiled. "I was really happy to see you come when you did."

His father's face clouded over. "I may not have been there to protect you all those years, my son, but nobody is going to hurt you now."

Though Thad knew it was dangerous, he still felt drawn back to the guest room in the back corner. He stood just outside the doorway, listening. "How could this happen to me?" Saul moaned softly. "I'm an honored man, a member of the Sanhedrin. I trained under Gamaliel, the grandson of Hillel and the Pharisee of Pharisees. I could hold my own against the best of them. How could I end up like this?

"I thought that Stephen's claim that he saw Yeshua standing at the right hand of Jehovah God was blasphemy. Yet now I've seen Him too. What am I going to do now? I've seen the risen Lord. I might as well die."

Before Thaddeus realized what he was doing, he had slipped around the corner and into the room. "You don't have to die," he said softly. "And I did see Him too. Do you want to hear about it?"

Saul stopped rocking. "Yes," he said after a moment.

"When I was a little boy, my father became possessed by a demon," Thaddeus began. "He was violent and no one could do anything with him. He and another man ended up living like animals in the graveyards outside of our town."

"Where did you live?" the Pharisee demanded.

"In Gadara."

The blind man raised an eyebrow. "Your father was one of the demoniacs of Gadara? I had heard they got pushed off a cliff where all those pigs died."

Thaddeus laughed. "We were afraid they were going to do that and they threatened to, but they let us leave town instead. Because my uncle owns this inn we came here. I don't know where the other man and his family went."

So *you* saw Yeshua, the risen Lord."

"Well, sort of," said Thad. "He wasn't risen then because He hadn't died yet."

Saul slowly sat up and nodded. "True, that would have been before then. So why were you sneaking up on Him, for surely you must have done that to catch Him in His undergarments. Of course, you are pretty good at slipping up on people. You've been doing it to me."

"No! No!" the boy protested. "I didn't. When He cast the demons out of my father and his friend, they were naked. They'd been running without clothes like wild animals for years. The first thing He did was to take off His robe and put it around my father, and He made one of His disciples take off his for the other man. They sent me back to the village to get some of my father's clothes. Yeshua cared about his dignity and was willing to stand there in His undergarments, waiting for me to return from town, so that my father wouldn't have to be embarrassed by being naked in front of everyone after Yeshua healed his mind."

Thaddeus choked up and could hardly speak. "It was the first time I had ever seen anyone care about my father—except for my mother."

"So you and your family are loyal followers of His?" Saul said slowly.

Thaddeus felt a sinking sensation in the pit of his stomach.

What if it was all a trick? What if the Slayer was sitting here pretending to be blind and sick, and he had just betrayed his entire family to the Sanhedrin's agent? His legs staggered as he slid down the wall and sat on the floor.

"Afraid to answer, are you? After all that the risen Lord did for your father, you're not even willing to answer me."

"Are you going to kill us?"

The little man let out a moan and started to rock, holding his head in his hands again. "Ah, whatever am I going to do? What am I going to do?" he mumbled.

Shakily the boy scrambled to his feet and raced out of the room as fast as he could.

A loud thudding began on the front gate. Father lifted the bar, opened the gate, and then whispered, "Ananias, what are you doing here? It's not safe. You must leave. We can meet another time for whatever you need to discuss."

The man shook his head. "No, God sent me here."

"Yes, yes," said father, "I know. He's sent us all here. But really this is not a good time. Please leave."

Ananias smiled grimly. "I don't feel any more comfortable about this than you do," he said. "But the Lord told me who your guest is, and I must speak with him."

"He's going to be the death of all of us," Father replied. "Thaddeus has already been on the receiving end of his fist."

The visitor glanced over at the boy and his bruised eye. "I know he's dangerous, but the Lord told me to come. I have to do this."

"If you must, then let us come with you."

The three walked into Saul's chamber. He had stopped rocking back and forth and was curled back up in his old position on the floor.

"Brother Saul," Ananias said, "the Lord has sent me to heal you of your blindness and to tell you that He has called you to minister to the Gentiles. He will be teaching you in the next few days the things you must know and the things you will have to endure in His service."

By now the Pharisee was sitting upright on the floor. Ananias put his hand on Saul's head.

Just then the Pharisee gave a sharp gasp. "I can see!" he cried. "I can see you! It's as if something like scales just fell off my eyes. I thought I was going to be blind the rest of my life." He looked around at Thaddeus and the two older men. "Thank you. Oh, thank you!" He stood.

"You have much to learn," Ananias said. "Don't you want to sit down?"

"No, I feel wonderful!" Saul protested. "I've met the risen Lord, and now I've been healed. I need to go tell everyone. Where's the nearest synagogue?"

Ananias shook his head. "You must be very careful, Brother Saul."

"Are you sure you want to call him Brother Saul?" Thaddeus's father whispered. "I mean, are we sure—yet?"

"The Lord has healed his blindness," Ananias replied softly. "I'm sure He has work for him and knows what He's doing."

"Will you direct me to the nearest synagogue?" Saul repeated to the boy.

"Brother Saul," Ananias interrupted, "you must be very careful. There are many who would like to see the followers of the risen Christ imprisoned and killed. Truly we thought that was why you came here to Damascus."

"Yes," Saul said sadly, "it was."

"I knew it," Thaddeus's father declared.

"But I met Him on the way."

Ananias raised an eyebrow. "Then you must be very careful for your safety. Going to the synagogue and preaching may make those there want to kill you too."

"Nonsense," the little man insisted. "Not when they hear who I am. I am Saul of the Sanhedrin, a Pharisee, trained under Gamaliel, grandson of Hillel."

"Yes, yes, we know all that," Ananias assured him. "Just be careful. The Lord said He was going to be sending you to the Gentiles."

Saul seemed to shrink within himself. "I would much rather preach at the local synagogue."

"Yes, I'm sure you would," Thaddeus's father observed. "You Pharisees avoid associating with Gentiles if at all possible."

"Surely you're not going to let Gentiles into your group!" Saul looked pointedly at Ananias and Thaddeus's father.

Ananias shrugged, and Father looked at the floor.

"You have Gentiles among you already?"

"Until recently," Ananias explained, "I had no great love for Gentiles either. But, well, Philip made his trip into Samaria, and many Samaritans have become believers. If they accept Yeshua . . ."

"Samaritans!" Saul exploded. "I hated the believers to start with. The fact that they'll accept Samaritans into their group . . . oh, it's a good thing I didn't know that before now."

"Well," Ananias continued, "you'll be safer preaching to the Samaritans than you would be to Jews around here."

Saul paused for a moment. "Yes," he said, "I do have much to learn. I have heard that Matthew, one of the 12, is living here in Damascus, or at least close to here. Could you take me to him?"

Father laughed. "Not a chance. We have risked our lives caring for your needs and giving you hospitality and answering your questions honestly. Ananias put his life in jeopardy because the Lord sent him here to heal you of your blindness and to tell you what His plans are for you. Now, you can be a follower of the risen Lord without being friends with me and my family, and you can certainly be a follower of the risen Lord without ever meeting Matthew. We will *not* divulge his hiding place to you."

"You are right," he said after a long pause. "I do have much to learn, but I will not impose on your hospitality any further. I thank you for caring for me during the time of my blindness, and whether or not you believe me, I will serve Yeshua Hamishea in whatever way He shows me."

"Where will you go? You have no money," Thaddeus blurted.

"My father did not leave me helpless," Saul said, quickly suppressing his frustration. "He made sure all of his sons learned a practical trade in addition to our religious schooling. I'm a skilled tentmaker. If you will direct me to the part of the city where the tentmakers live, I shall earn my keep there."

Father nodded. "Well, you will get to know the Gentiles then, because that's the people you'll be staying with. If you follow this road. . . ." He led Saul out of the courtyard and pointed him in the direction of the city's tentmakers. "It will be quite a walk," he cautioned him. "The tentmakers are on the outskirts of town on the other side. But if you just follow Straight Street, this road right here, it goes all the way through."

"I thank you," he said awkwardly. "And I pray the blessings of the risen Yeshua Hamishea on you." He said it awkwardly, as if it were the first time it had ever passed his lips.

"I will go with you," Ananias volunteered. Saul stared at him for a moment, then nodded. "Good!" he said. "You can baptize me at the river."

Thaddeus's mouth dropped open in shock, but Ananias answered smoothly, "Of course." And the two headed for the other side of town.

"Are we safe?" Thaddeus asked breathlessly.

His father put his arm around him. "As safe as we've ever been," he said slowly. "No one on the face of the earth is ever totally safe. Yet surely Father God would not have restored the sight of this Pharisee so that he could kill us."

* * *

Thaddeus scooped his sister, Helena, up onto his shoulders. "Come on, baby," he said. "Do you need a ride?"

Helena squealed with glee and dug her chubby fingers into his curly hair to hang on for balance. Her brother jogged across the courtyard, causing her shrieks of joy to come out in little bursts as she bounced on his neck.

When he stopped she screamed, "More, more! Go! Go!"

Suddenly he heard someone knocking. He carried his sister over to the door of the family courtyard and cautiously peered out. Then he quickly opened it and pulled the man in from the street.

"Saul, what are you doing here? It's dangerous. Why did you come back? We heard you had left town and gone to the deserts of Arabia."

"I did, and I've been out there for a long time."

The young man nodded. "Yes, long enough for me to have a little sister."

"Go! Go!" Helena screamed.

"Just a minute, baby," Thaddeus said. "Sit still." He held on to her ankles carefully so that she couldn't fall as she bounced wildly, trying to get him to carry her around some more.

"I thought I'd been gone long enough," Saul continued. "Someone needs to preach the truth here in Damascus, and well, I've spent a lot of time with the Lord and preached to a lot of Gentiles. And I decided that it's been long enough that people will have forgotten how angry they were at me."

"I don't think they have," Thaddeus murmured.

"Well, I thought I'd stop by and say hello to you. I'm not planning to stay here at your family inn, so I won't bring any danger to you. I will lodge in the tentmakers' part of town. I still have a few friends there, I think."

"I hope you're right, Saul. I hope you're right."

"Well, it's good to see you. I'll be leaving now. And I'm glad to see that your little sister is growing strong and healthy."

Thaddeus smiled.

"Go! Go!" Helena persisted.

With a nod at Saul, Thaddeus again trotted his sister around on his shoulders.

Stepping out into the street, Saul closed the gate behind him, and Thaddeus continued to play with his baby sister.

Only a few days later Saul knocked at the gate again. This time Thaddeus's father let him in and quickly shut it behind him.

In a few moments a group of angry men strode down the street past the closed gate. "He came this way; I saw him," one of them shouted.

Thaddeus's eyes widened. He motioned to Saul to step over to the part of the courtyard they had devoted to basket weaving. *Saul was not a tall man for having such a reputation in his past,* he thought. Quickly he took the lid off one of their largest storage baskets, one they had just finished that week. He motioned for the reformed persecutor to climb into the basket, and then slapped the lid back on. It was just in time.

The group banged on the gate, and Father opened it.

"We're looking for that exiled Pharisee who came back. Have you seen him?"

"You're welcome to look around here," Father told them. "We have no guests in the inn this early in the day."

The men swarmed around the courtyard and peered cautiously into the family rooms and storage rooms. Finding nothing, they said, "If you see him, let us know."

Uncle Judas nodded. "I certainly will."

Thaddeus scowled. How could his uncle promise something like that? Picking up his sister, he held her tight. His mother sat in the basketry nook, weaving baskets as she did many hours a day. She also said nothing.

The men left, and Thaddeus's father and Uncle Judas closed and barred the gate.

"What are we going to do?" Thaddeus whispered to his father. "Will Uncle really tell them?"

His father shook his head. "No. But your uncle didn't see him. I just told him what we were doing. Uncle Judas will stay out of the way and avoid any contact with him. He promised the men he would tell them if he saw him, but so far he hasn't seen him."

A sick feeling in his stomach, Thaddeus shook his head. He hugged his little sister tight until she squirmed to get down. Had he brought danger to her because of his friendship with the ex-Pharisee? Closing his eyes, he leaned against the wall.

"God of Israel," he whispered, "and God of Damascus and the God who healed my father, help me know what to do now. Please don't let my family be hurt because of something I did. Please give me wisdom and help us. I can't believe that You would want my friend Saul to die when he loves you so much. And my family loves You too, except for Helena, who is too young. But she would if she ever met You. I remember what Yeshua was like with children." Then he smiled to himself.

Suddenly he realized that he was smiling in his prayer instead of pleading for help. A feeling of warmth seemed to spread its glow through him and take away the fear in the pit of his stomach. Running to his father, he said, "I have an idea." Then he whispered with his father for several minutes.

His father nodded. "Tonight. Meanwhile, we need to keep everything quiet and as normal as possible here."

They moved the large basket in which Paul hid into their private family quarters so that no one in the courtyard or the inn would see it.

Mother showed up moments later with food and a small jug of water. "Here," she told Saul. "You must stay hidden, because the evening guests will arrive and want to get settled by sundown. Until then you must be quiet and remain back here. There will be many people milling around the courtyard with their animals, and it will be noisy. But you must stay out of sight. Too many people know who you are. We will help you escape later in the night, when everyone is asleep."

"But how?" he asked.

"It's best we don't talk right now. The less said, the better. Eat and try to rest, for you're going to be traveling most of the night."

Thaddeus smiled as a thought struck him. Had God provided the reeds and his mother's previous basket weaving skills just to support their family when they had arrived with no way to make a living, or had it all been part of a plan formed a long time ago so that they would have big storage baskets so that they could hide Saul and help him escape? Finally he shrugged.

I smiled. Every once in a while humans have a little glimpse of the intricate plans the Almighty has made for their lives. And they get just a peak into the gentle care and attention to detail that He puts in to their preparations years beforehand to care for them during times of need.

For now Thaddeus may forget his little glimpse, but time and again throughout his life he will continue to see more of them. Yet it won't be until he joins the Mighty One and Yeshua in Their heavenly home, and discovers what really was happening during all of those times, that he will grasp all that He did for him. Until then, he remains loyal to his God despite the fact that he does not understand the Creator's working.

*　*　*

By midnight everyone in the courtyard seemed asleep. The animals had settled down. The campfires were just faintly glowing coals in the darkness.

Thaddeus's father helped Saul out of the basket. "Stretch your legs," he said, "and do what you need to, then follow us up to the roof." Then he and his son carried the basket up to the roof. Mother brought a small packet that she put into the basket. "Bread and dried fruit for his journey," she said. "He'll need it. And some water." She placed a small waterskin in next to it.

Saul followed them up and climbed obediently back into the basket. Thaddeus and his father and mother carefully tied ropes around it so that they could safely lower it.

"It's fortunate that we live right on the city wall," Father commented, "although that's the logical place to have an inn. There are men guarding the gates at both ends of the city, so do not go by the main road. As soon as you get out of the basket, head off into the desert and don't come back here. Our people have a long memory."

"God bless you and your family for your kindness to me," Saul said.

Father's voice softened. "And may He also bless you and take you safely wherever you must go."

Reaching over, Saul gently squeezed Thaddeus's shoulder. "And God bless you especially," he said. "He has great plans for your life."

The younger man smiled. Then he and his mother and father gently lowered the basket over the wall. It reached the ground with a soft thud. And it was only moments before they felt the three tugs on the rope, their sign to pull it back up. Quickly they coiled the rope back up and tossed it into the corner on the roof where it had been before and carried the basket back down the steps and inside their home. No sign now remained that anything unusual had happened.

"Thank You, Father God," Thaddeus whispered. "And thank You, Yeshua, my Friend and my God."

"Amen," his father added.

"Oh, I didn't realize that I said that out loud."

His father hugged him. "It's all right. I'm thankful too."

Portia

(Caesarea)

 was delighted to discover that my next assignment in Caesarea was the daughter of one of my previous charges, Antonia. She had been married to the centurion Cornelius during the time that she was a special favorite of Portia, wife of Pilate, governor of Judea. And while it was usually unheard-of for a Roman soldier to marry, Cornelius had been approaching the end of his term of service and was a special favorite because he was a good man, trusted both by the people he served and by those he governed. His men under him were all loyal Romans. They were the elite guard of the Roman cohort and respected and looked up to.

Cornelius and Antonia had a modest home by Roman standards in Caesarea, with servants and a headstrong young daughter who was to be my charge. As I approached my new assignment I rapidly reviewed her life experiences. She had the strength and tenacity of her mother and the leadership qualities of her father all bundled into one energetic adolescent. I smiled as I looked at her great potential.

At the time her parents were sitting in the courtyard under an awning to shade them from the afternoon sun.

"I'm really worried about Portia," Antonia said to her husband.

Cornelius sighed. "She certainly has spirit, doesn't she?"

"Spirit is fine. I had spirit. It's just that—she's uncontrollable."

He laughed. "And you weren't?"

She sighed. "I'm sure part of it is just a problem of whom she associates with. After all, she has no brothers and sisters."

As soon as she said it she stared dejectedly at her feet. Cornelius put his arm around her.

"She may still," he said.

"I know," his wife replied sadly. "But she spends all her time gossiping with the servants and any traders that come into town. You would think that she wants to rule the world, the way she collects news and gossip from everyone. I thought most young girls liked to go to the market to see the soaps and the jewels and the things brought from the East and from Rome and to find out what the fashions are elsewhere. Not our daughter—she wants to talk to the traders. She asks all kinds of questions and would never buy a thing if I wasn't along to pick out one or two things to save us from total embarrassment. It's not proper."

"What would you have her do?" Cornelius asked. "Jewish families would never consider her as an appropriate friend of their daughters, so that leaves the local Gentiles. And none of them are aristocrats—they're not going to teach her proper Roman manners. You're going to have to do that."

"I don't even know them all," Antonia protested. "I've spent most of my life here in Judea too, being Roman but not knowing Roman culture very well. And definitely not being Jewish, either."

Her husband shook his head. "Well, at least we associate with some Romans because of my job position. Caesarea at least has a large Gentile population. However, since most soldiers don't marry, the Roman young people Antonia's age are just the offspring of soldiers and their concubines. And she's not going to learn the culture you want from them. Sometimes I think she's better off talking to the merchants in the market."

Antonia sighed. "We will pray about it, Cornelius."

"Surely if the God of heaven cared enough to take care of you in your unusual upbringing and bring you to me, He can take care of Portia, too."

She shrugged. "Perhaps the God of heaven is more patient than I am."

"Or else not as finicky." He laughed. "Or maybe," he suggested, "the God of heaven hasn't finished with our daughter yet."

His wife smiled. "I suppose. I used to believe so strongly in Him, and I used to believe that the Yeshua crucified at that Passover was His Son. But that was so long, and now I don't know what I believe. I keep asking Him for more children."

"At least He gave us Portia," Cornelius pointed out.

"Yes," she agreed, "He did give us Portia."

Antonia stood and walked back into the house. Once she left, Cornelius's shoulders sagged. He was a tough Roman centurion, but he loved his wife, and it broke his heart to see her feeling sad. He too had prayed for more children. But he didn't know what more he could do at this point. Finally he headed for the stables. It was a likely place to find Portia. "Portia," he called out, "are you in here?"

"Father, I'm down at this end. Come see this foal."

His long stride quickly brought him to where his daughter was. "Isn't she beautiful?"

Cornelius nodded. "She is."

"And look, she likes me."

Her father laughed. "Most horses like you if you pet and fuss over them the way you do. I think every horse in this stable likes you, but you must not come here without a servant with you. It's not safe."

"But Father," she protested, "everybody knows that I'm your

daughter. Nobody's going to touch me, because they're all scared of you. You're in charge here."

"There are six centurions here in Caesarea and other more important people. You seem to think that I'm emperor of the entire universe even though I keep trying to tell you that my powers don't stretch quite that far."

Portia flung her arms around him. "Well, you're king of my world."

Cornelius tried to keep his face impassive and stare straight ahead, but he couldn't prevent the smile playing around the corners of his mouth. Who could resist such adoration? He scooped her up in his arms and hugged her.

"And you and your mother are the center of my world," he replied. "But you still can't come out here without a servant with you. You're going to have to stay home for a week if I catch you running off alone again. Do you understand?"

"Then put me down. Don't hug me and threaten me at the same time."

Cornelius set her back on the ground. "It's because I love you," he said. "There's no one else in the world that I threaten and hug at the same time."

As he stood with his hands on his hips he suddenly looked very tall to Portia. "I'll try to remember, Father. But it's not my fault if the servants are so slow that they just don't keep up with me in the marketplace."

"Yes, it is, Portia. You will stay with a servant when outside the family quarters. And you will apologize for worrying your mother to death."

"I didn't mean to scare Mother. She should know that I'm fine."

"Yes, yes, I know you're the daughter of Cornelius," he echoed. "Now let's get you back home."

He tried to shorten his stride so that his daughter could keep up with him as they headed back to the house.

"So did you talk to anyone interesting today?" he asked.

"Oh, yes. There was a merchant who had come through Lydda last. He says that Peter, the Christian fisherman, was there. Peter was one of the twelve, you know—of that group."

"Yes, I'm aware of who that particular Peter the fisherman is."

"Well," she continued importantly, "he was in Lydda a few days ago, and there was a man named Aeneas who was really sick. Everybody thought he was going to die. Peter came in and laid his hands on him and told him to get up and be better, probably in the name of Jesus, because that's what he does in all the stories about him."

"Yes, I've heard some of them."

"Well, anyway, the man named Aeneas got up. It must be a true story, because the merchant who came through said he was there when it happened. So it's not something that somebody who knew somebody else who knew somebody else told him. He really saw it."

"Interesting," her father said.

"Well, do you believe it?"

"I don't know. Perhaps. There are a lot of wild stories floating around, but every once in a while you encounter a few true ones."

"I've heard a lot of stories about this Peter. People bring their sick family members to him, and if his shadow touches them, they get better. And some of them take handkerchiefs for him to touch, and then they go home with them to their sick family members and they are healed."

Cornelius laughed. "Yes, the marketplace is always full of tales. But there are still lots of sick people in this country."

"Maybe Peter hasn't gotten around to all of them yet. Or perhaps he heals only the ones that actually believe."

"That could be," her father said after thinking about it for a moment.

"Wouldn't it be fun to check him out?"

"No," Cornelius said. "And besides, Roman centurions don't do anything for fun, remember?"

"Sure you do. When you're with me it's fun, isn't it?"

He smiled at her. "Yes, it is, but we're not going to Lydda to try to find this Peter person. We're going to stay right here in Caesarea, except that I will go wherever my cohort gets sent. And you will stay home and not go adventuring even outside the family courtyard without a servant anymore, remember?"

Portia hung her head.

Only days later she was bursting with news again. "Mother, Father, do you know what that Peter has done now?"

Antonia rolled her eyes. "There's no telling."

Portia laughed. "It's even better than the Aeneas story. And—and I even took a servant *with* me when I went to the market today."

"Yes, you did. That was good," her father said. "So what did you hear?"

"Well, rumor has it that Peter is in Joppa now. And there was this woman named Dorcas there. I guess she was pretty wealthy. And she took care of a lot of the other widows and children of the widows. She made them all clothes and helped them with food and things like that."

"Yes, there are some very kind wealthy widows out there," her mother commented.

"Well, she was one," Portia continued, "and she got really sick and died. And the people were so sad, and they dragged her upstairs to their little room up on the roof, and the women had all bathed her and gotten ready to bury her."

"Yes, that's their custom here," Antonia observed. "Remember that Jews bury somebody the same day that that person dies."

"Well, they sent for Peter, because he wasn't too far away from Joppa at the time."

"What did Peter do?" her mother asked. "Finish up the sewing that she hadn't quite gotten done, or just miraculously feed all the widows by multiplying the leftover bread in the kitchen?"

"Oh, Mother, don't be so sarcastic. He did something far better than that—he raised her back to life, and she came back downstairs and resumed what she was doing. The man in the market says that she looks just the way she did before and just as healthy as can be. Doesn't even act tired."

Antonia shook her head. "They're just stories. I wish you wouldn't gossip with people like that."

"Mother," the girl protested, "what if it's true?"

"I don't believe it. Peter was a follower of Yeshua of Nazareth, but I wasn't very impressed with him."

Cornelius nudged his wife gently. "It's been 10 or 12 years since then," he pointed out. "Maybe the man has changed."

His wife raised an eyebrow. "He cursed like every other fisherman back then," she said. "He's not anyone I would want to have around Portia."

Sophia, one of their servants, nodded as she set down a bowl of fruit on the table near the family. "Yes," she said, "I was in the courtyard when he was trying to convince us that he didn't know Yeshua of Nazareth. Such words. He would have made a good Roman sailor."

The woman had come to be Antonia's personal servant as a gift from Pilate's wife when the girl married Cornelius. It gave her a friend to talk to, though they rarely discussed the events of that horrifying Passover.

"Well," Portia decided, "I think that we should go check him out and find out if he's for real or not."

Sophia laughed. "He wouldn't talk to you anyway, Lady Portia. Gilgal the butcher says that Peter often said that he hates swine's flesh, onions, and Gentiles."

Portia wrinkled up her nose. "Well, I don't like onions either," she said, "so this Peter person can't be *all* bad."

"It may be," Cornelius said slowly, "that Peter has changed his view on Gentiles. The last intelligence update we had told us that the Christian groups are spreading. The biggest group of them right now is in Antioch in Syria, and I'm sure they're not all Jews there. We've also heard that Philip, one of the twelve, has been baptizing Gentiles, and some Pharisee (or he used to be one, anyway) named Saul has also been baptizing Gentiles. So Peter may need to alter his views."

"Or maybe he already has," Portia suggested. "You know, people sometimes do change."

Antonia shook her head. "I don't know. He didn't seem like a very loyal follower to me, and I haven't seen anything of him since—and these stories are way too far-fetched to be true. Though if they were, it sounds as if he's not all bad."

She ended the conversation by standing to her feet and walking back into the kitchen with Sophia.

"Father," Portia said, "if we can't go see Peter, what if you invited him here?"

Cornelius smiled. "I could do that, but I don't think he would come."

"Why not? You're a centurion. He has to do what you say."

"I'm hardly going to force him to be a guest in my house. I have found that if you're going to be successful in life, it's best to compel people to do only what you feel they must do, and not use your power for personal curiosity."

"Well, couldn't we at least invite him?" she persisted. "He can only say no. Besides, he might not be that strict of a Jew anymore. After all, he's staying at the house of Simon the tanner, and you know how some Jews feel about tanners."

Her father's mouth dropped open. "How did you know where he was staying?"

"Oh, I hear things. Although I don't know why anybody who

used to be a fisherman would care about the way a tannery smells. I think fishermen smell bad too."

Cornelius laughed. "I'd have to agree with you there."

"So do you think you might invite him?"

After looking at his daughter for a long time, he said, "I will send two servants. While I will not command him to come, I will invite him as a guest. If he refuses, you must not be disappointed. No one can understand these people."

"If he refuses to come, I promise not to be disappointed out loud."

"Well, I guess that's the best you can do," her father said with a laugh. Then as he walked away, he mumbled, "I am going to be in such trouble with your mother."

The next few days seemed to drag for Portia.

"Remember that Joppa is an overnight trip and my servants will probably have to stay overnight on the way back too," Cornelius reminded her at one point. "Don't be impatient."

I wondered how the Mighty One was going to handle this stubborn apostle of His. The last time I had had contact with Peter (and from what I had heard from other angels) he was pretty unhappy about the growing influence of Gentiles among the believers. He felt they should be in a separate class from Jewish believers. And he had a real problem imagining any of them in a leadership role. I smiled. Yeshua had handled Peter many times before, and I knew that He and His Father would come up with something. I couldn't wait to see what.

It was late afternoon as the two servants and their guest arrived at the centurion's home. They escorted the big fisherman in through the gate. Antonia appeared in the doorway to welcome Peter.

One of the servants briefly bowed his head and announced, "This is Peter the fisherman from Capernaum."

She eyed him suspiciously. "And you are here because . . ."

"Your husband sent for me."

"Please have a seat," Antonia said reluctantly. "My husband will return from his duties in an hour or so. The servants will help you get refreshed, and I will send some bread and fruit to you. You must be hungry. When my husband arrives, we will have dinner."

Peter followed the servants as instructed.

After he had washed and relaxed for a moment, Portia appeared.

"Hello. My name is Portia. I have a lot of things I need to ask you."

The bearded Jew looked up at her, surprised.

"Well, I've heard so many things, and I have to find out if they're true."

The fisherman looked amused, then said awkwardly, "I'm not really accustomed to speaking to women without the man of her house being present."

"Oh well, that shouldn't be a problem. I bet you're not accustomed to eating at the house of a Gentile anyway, are you now?"

The fisherman broke into an embarrassed smile. "You know a lot for one so young."

"Oh, I'm not so young. I'm 12 years old. That's long enough to know a lot of things."

"I guess it is," he said slowly.

"So is the Aeneas story true?"

"It depends what you've heard."

"Well, we heard that he was very sick and practically dead and . . ."

"Well, he wasn't dead yet."

"And you healed him."

"No, actually I didn't."

"Well, everyone says you did."

"Yeshua of Nazareth healed him."

"But I thought Yeshua died a long time ago. I mean, I know you're a follower of His and everything."

"He died, but He lives," Peter explained. "He was raised back to life."

"That's great," she blurted. "That just proves it can be done. So does that mean the Dorcas story is true too?"

Peter broke into a laugh. "Yes, Dorcas was raised to life also by the power of Yeshua, not by any power I have."

"So it is true!" she exclaimed. "My father will love talking to you."

Peter tensed and looked nervously around.

"Don't worry," she said. "He's not planning to hurt you."

Antonia entered the room. "Portia, go to the kitchen and stop bothering our guest."

"She was not a bother," Peter protested.

"He hasn't cursed once," the girl said.

Peter and Antonia both looked embarrassed. "I don't do that anymore," he said.

Portia looked disappointed.

"She can listen when you talk to her father," her mother explained.

Peter nodded, looking a little more comfortable. Portia frowned and followed her mother glumly out to the kitchen.

"I hope Father comes home soon," she muttered.

It seemed like hours until Cornelius returned home that evening. Portia raced out to meet him.

"Father, he's here! He's here! And the stories are true. At least he says they are. But Mother won't let me talk to him by myself. I'm so glad you're home!"

"Good," her father managed to get in. "I'm glad to be home too." He sniffed appreciatively. "It smells wonderful in here. What is your mother cooking?"

"I don't know for sure," said Portia. "I wasn't paying attention, but you can be pretty sure it's not swine's flesh, onions, or Gentiles."

Cornelius laughed. "Apparently Gentiles aren't so bad. Perhaps we could teach him to eat onions, too."

"Maybe him, but not me," she said stubbornly.

Portia endured the appropriate introductions and mealtime

small talk. After all, well-bred people did not jump feet first into the kind of conversation she wanted. Eventually her father and their visitor got around to the point of the visit.

"I was not sure you would come," Cornelius commented.

"You sent for me," the fisherman said respectfully. "You are a centurion, part of the occupying force in my country. Did I have a choice?"

Cornelius frowned. "My servants had been instructed specifically to make sure that you knew you had a choice. I asked that you come as my guest."

"Yes, yes, they did not fail in their duties. I just was rather surprised that you would invite me to your home, since I'm a Jew."

"As surprised as I was that you came?"

Peter looked embarrassed. "What prompted you to invite me?"

"An angel told me to when I was praying," Cornelius said after a pause. "I have great respect for your God, although I do not associate with other believers . . . being who I am . . ."

"An angel told you?" Portia blurted. "I'm not an angel."

Everyone laughed, Peter somewhat nervously.

"No, you're not an angel," her father agreed. He turned to Peter. "My daughter also wanted to meet you."

Peter smiled. "And we have met."

"Yes, and apparently you and my wife have also met before."

The fisherman paled and stared at Antonia. "I don't recall," he said after a pause.

"It's all right," the centurion reassured him. "She was a child then, about the age of my Portia. Yeshua of Nazareth healed her father's servant. She has held Him in high regard since then."

"I see. So you're the centurion's daughter from Capernaum?"

Antonia nodded stiffly.

"Apparently your respect for my Master does not extend to me," he said slowly.

"That's because Mother thinks that you weren't a very loyal follower of His to run away and leave Him all alone when He was killed that time."

"Portia," her mother snapped, "if you want to be a part of this discussion, you're going to have to sit and listen and not speak so often."

The fisherman colored. He turned to Portia. "I did not know your mother was there, but it is true. I was very afraid and ran away. And when He was brought to trial, I slipped into the courtyard to see what was going on."

Sophia stood behind Antonia, nodding her head. Suddenly recognition crossed Peter's face. "And you—you were there."

"Yes, I was," the servant woman said.

"And you spoke to me in the courtyard."

Another nod.

Peter put his face in his hands. "It will follow me all the days of my life wherever I go. There's always someone who remembers my cowardice. It is my Lord who is good, not me. And any good things that I do are just in His name."

"Well, at least you claim to know Him now," Sophia observed.

Peter sighed. "Yes," he said. "When you asked me last time, I claimed not to know Him."

"Is that when you did all the cursing?" Portia asked.

Becoming redder by the minute, Peter nodded. "This is embarrassing. I do so want you to respect my Lord, and yet my behavior has made it so that you won't even listen to me."

"Don't be too sure of that," Cornelius said, "and don't be too embarrassed. It's been many years. And we sent for you because we want to know more about Him. And more about you and the fellowship of other believers. According to what I hear large groups of believers are forming all over the empire, and it is no longer just among Jews. We were wondering . . ."

Antonia glanced at him, and he stopped.

"So tell us what made you willing to come here," Cornelius said a moment later.

The color that had been receding down Peter's neck now flooded back into his face again. "Oh, that's embarrassing too. But I will tell you everything. I was up on the roof of the house I was staying at—"

"Simon the tanner's?" Portia interrupted.

"Yes. It was afternoon, and I was taking a nap in the shade up on the roof."

Portia grinned. "And we know how fishermen love their afternoon naps."

"Yes, I guess it's force of habit. We do our work very early in the day and are exhausted by afternoon."

"Yes, yes," Cornelius urged. "You were sleeping. And my men awakened you?"

"No, but I had the strangest dream. At first I thought perhaps the fumes of the tanner were finally getting to me."

"They would certainly get to me," Portia began, then fell silent at a sharp look from her mother.

"It was as if a large sheet was let down from heaven with ropes tied to the corners, and the Lord told me to look in and I did. It was full of all kinds of ritually unclean animals. Do you know which ones are unclean? Probably not, since you're not Jewish. They're all animals that Jewish people would not eat. Swine, camels, owls, any beasts of prey. And the Lord said, 'Arise, kill and eat.' I was horrified."

Portia started to laugh.

"I have never eaten ritually unclean meat in my entire life. Good Jews are willing to die rather than to eat such meat. I was even sure this message was not from God."

"But it must have been," the girl interrupted. "My father and I both prayed about it."

Everyone turned in surprise to Portia. "You pray?"

It was her turn to color. "Um, to the one God. I just never told anyone before."

"Really?" her father asked with interest. "Did your mother teach you that?."

"Mother prays to the one God?" the girl said in surprise.

Antonia blushed.

"Well," Peter commented, "it is becoming more apparent to me what the Lord was talking about."

"When?" Antonia demanded.

"Well, after I refused to kill and eat any of the animals He had offered me, He said, 'What God has made clean, do not call unclean.' And right at that moment I heard your servants calling me from down below. They were very polite and did not try to enter the home, which was kind of them."

Cornelius nodded. "Yes, they were ordered not to make you feel uncomfortable or defiled. They were just to invite you."

"As they did. You and your family obviously have respect for the Lord. Perhaps He was telling me that He has made you clean and that I have no right to be prejudiced against you even though you are not Jews."

Portia laughed merrily. "We're Romans."

Everyone nodded.

"Welcome to Yeshua's family," Peter said after thinking a moment. "You were there that weekend." He turned to Antonia. "You remember the crucifixion?"

The woman shuddered. "It was horrible—just horrible. Portia and I went down to the cross. Not my daughter Portia, but Pilate's wife. We named her after the governor's wife."

"You were at the cross?" Peter asked in surprise. "Then you were closer to Him than I was when He died. You know that He came back to life again?"

Antonia nodded.

"I remember the soldiers accepting bribes to tell people that His body was stolen in the night. Now we are trying to tell everyone about Him. Our prophetic books told us that He was coming, that He would arrive as the Lamb of God and take away our sins."

"Oh, like the Jewish people's sacrifices?" Portia said.

"Exactly."

"What do you know about Jewish religion?" Antonia said, turning to her daughter.

"Oh, I hear things."

Her mother shook her head.

"It is good," Peter commented. "If you understand the Jewish sacrifices, then you understand who Yeshua was and why He had to die. And why it gives us such freedom, since now we can pray directly to God because He has made us clean. Now God treats us as Yeshua deserves because Yeshua was treated as we deserve—"

"So His death was not a huge tragedy?" Antonia interrupted. "Not a terrible mistake?"

"It was terrible. They were so cruel to Him. But He allowed that to happen because He traded His life for ours."

Peter and Cornelius and the family sat and talked late into the evening. The centurion shook his head in wonder. "All these years I have been a believer in the one God. Antonia was in Jerusalem the week of the crucifixion of Yeshua of Nazareth. And we believed He was the Son of the one God, but we never could understand why He was killed. Finally it all fits together. It makes sense."

"I was one of His disciples," Peter said, "yet it was not until some time after He was crucified that it made sense to me, either. Isn't it wonderful the way God put His plan together and offered to pay for the sins not only of Jews, but of anyone who believes on Him?"

"May we be baptized the way you baptize Jewish believers?" Antonia requested.

"Absolutely. Anyone who is willing to repent and believe on the

Lord Jesus Christ can be baptized. And you even have water right here." He glanced toward the ornamental fish pond with its fountain at one end.

Peter baptized Cornelius, Antonia, their daughter, and all of the servants. Even old Petronius hobbled out and insisted on climbing over the stone wall into the water himself.

As Antonia stood dripping and laughing, she said, "Now we are a whole family of baptized believers. What do you think will happen next?"

"I don't know," Cornelius said, putting his arm around her, "but I imagine it will be exciting."

The years to come would indeed be exciting, and I would get to record some of it.

Jonathan ben Doud

(Jerusalem)

Here, Jonathan," his father said. "This is the last tray of cakes to go up the stairs. And be careful. You know Martha wants everything perfect."

The boy laughed. His stepmother always wanted everything to be perfect. That was just part of who she was. He glanced over at her as she stood in the doorway, her hands on the small of her back. It was the closest that she ever came to complaining of a backache. The fullness of her robes hid the swelling of her body, but Jonathan knew his stepmother was expecting another little one. Being as protective as possible, he and his father tried not to let her carry anything heavy or to overwork herself, which was hard to prevent because Martha was the busiest woman he had ever known in his life.

Although unable to recall his birth mother, he did remember the day that he and his father had met Martha. It was the worst and best day of his short life. The worst because it was the day of the crucifixion. Yeshua had healed his father and his grandfather of leprosy and had triumphantly ridden Jonathan's own donkey into Jerusalem. And a week later He was being crucified. And yet that had been where they had met Martha.

Martha, who had scooped Jonathan up in her arms, fussed and scolded his father for bringing such a small child to such a terrible event, then bustled around finding him something to eat and otherwise distracting him from the frightening scene until the darkness and the horrible earthquake began. Even in a time of such horrible suffering, Jehovah God had seen to his needs. And not just something to eat, but his lack of a mother.

Now he had two young brothers, two little sisters, and whoever this next member of the family would be.

The meeting of the believers was going to be very important. Martha had been preparing for it for some time, cooking and organizing. They were holding it in Jerusalem at the house of Mary, the mother of John Mark, for she had a home with a large upper room that she rented out for such occasions. It was the very room where Yeshua and His disciples had met for the last time before the crucifixion. And it was the place where the tiny band of Christians had waited for the falling of the Holy Spirit after Yeshua had gone back to His Father. Now it was going to be the room where the most important leaders of all the Christian churches would assemble. Representatives had come from Antioch and every other significant center of believers.

"Please let me stay for the meetings, Father," Jonathan begged. "I would give anything to see all these people I've heard so much about. Please let me stay. I'll sit quietly in the corner of the room."

His father smiled. "Not this time, Jonathan," he said. "I have a hunch that there'll be a fair amount of heated exchanges in this meeting."

"That won't bother me," his son protested.

His father shook his head.

"Do you have enough servants? I'll even be the greeter at the door and wash their feet as they come in."

Doud raised an eyebrow. "You want to be here that badly?"

Jonathan nodded.

The young man's father thought a moment. "Well, then you may be the servant in charge of the foot washing."

"Oh, thank you. Let me run down and get one more basket, and then I'll bring up the foot basins."

"And don't forget the water," his father added. "The foot washer hauls the water, too."

At first Jonathan didn't mind the foot washing as he strained to catch names and the places that people had come from. But then everyone started arriving at once. They all seemed concerned to have their needs taken care of first. Jonathan couldn't keep up with it all. Two of the men snapped at him because he was too slow. He felt the blood rushing to his face and knew that his ears were bright red and sticking straight out from the sides of his head like handles on a waterpot.

Just when he felt he was going to burst with frustration, a man knelt next to him and started washing the next pair of feet. He glanced over with appreciation and realized with horror that it was the apostle Peter.

"You can't do this," he whispered.

"Sure I can," the big fisherman whispered back. "I'll tell you why later. Yeshua did this once for me. The least I can do is do it for His friends."

Jonathan's mouth dropped open. Yeshua did this? Suddenly He felt as if he had the most important job in the room. Washing the dirty feet of the tired travelers was no longer frustrating.

I can't wait to hear Peter's story, he thought.

When they finished the last pair of feet, all the men took their seats. The apostles and those who seemed most important sat in an inner circle, with others in an outer circle around them. From his spot by the door Jonathan could see most of the guests, and he hoped they spoke loud enough that he wouldn't miss anything.

Before they even started the meeting, Nathan, from Antioch, loudly demanded, "Since when has church leadership allowed foot washers to sit on the inner circle?"

A chuckle rose from the inner circle. James ben Joseph, the one in charge of the meeting, replied, "Nathan, I would like you to meet Simon Peter."

Peter nodded in Nathan's direction, but a fit of coughing muffled the man's apology.

"Brothers, we need to get on with this meeting," James said, interrupting the amusement at Nathan's predicament. "It seems we have conflict among us and among our churches. We've met here with representatives from all of our church groups in order to settle this, so that we can handle things with unity."

A murmur spread through the delegates. "Since the gospel has been offered to Gentiles in addition to the Jews," James continued, "a number of questions have come up. Many Gentiles have been baptized and become followers of Yeshua and have received the Holy Spirit. Some of them have been told that they must also adopt our Jewish ceremonial laws and undergo circumcision before they can actually be saved."

"Amen!" several men said, vigorously nodding their approval.

Several others frowned and shook their heads. "No, that's not right."

Small discussions began to break out.

"Brethren," James said firmly, "you will all get an opportunity to present your opinion. But let us do it one at a time and with order here.

"The laws of Moses are important. They are what make us who we are. God gave them to us, and as the Scriptures say, 'I am Jehovah. I change not.' He doesn't change; neither should we. If these new Christians want to be saved, they need to keep the law that God honored us with. We received it through Moses, and it's more important than anything else we could teach Gentiles."

A short, bald man at the end of the inner circle shook his head violently. "It cannot be more important," he said firmly. "Jesus and Him crucified is the most important thing we can teach others. All of the things Moses taught us pointed forward to Jesus."

"Yeshua," corrected one of the Jewish delegates.

"Yes, Yeshua or Jesus, whichever name you want to use, for we have both Jews and Gentiles here. The only purposes for the laws of Moses were to point forward to the coming of Jesus, Yeshua, or else to care for the health and civilization of our people. Only Moses could have provided the discipline to make a civilized nation out of the band of slaves we were at the time our people left Egypt."

"Are you saying," Nathan blustered, "that Yeshua was more important than Moses?"

"Yes," the bald man replied emphatically, "that's exactly what I'm saying."

Murmuring and arguing broke out in the group again.

"I thought we'd settled this a long time ago," Peter interrupted. "I used to dislike Gentiles, and I was extremely careful not to associate with them, eat with them, or do anything that would make me ritually unclean. And yet several years ago when I was visiting Simon the tanner . . ."

"Jonathan," his father tapped him on the shoulder, "you're one of the servants, remember?"

His son jumped. He had been so involved with listening that he had forgotten his duties. "I'm sorry."

Doud smiled. "I understand, but you need to refill the cups."

As Jonathan ran down the steps as quickly as he could he remembered the story about Peter's vision. He wished he could have seen the look on the apostle's face when the Lord had told him to eat all of those strange animals in the sheet. Returning to the room, Jonathan moved quietly around it, taking care of people's empty drinking cups.

"To become Christians," another individual argued, "no one made us give up our culture and become Gentiles. We're still as Jewish as we ever were. So perhaps it is not right either for us to make Gentiles give up their culture and become Jewish. After all, what we are offering them is not conversion to Judaism but the good news about Yeshua, who came to save all of us from our sins."

"So maybe they can be saved," a Pharisee protested, "but surely they're going to be a different class of believer."

"No!" came a loud voice from the bald man at the end. "No separate classes. Not among the followers of Jesus. I was a better Pharisee than you. Yet I count all of that as nothing."

"Humph," Nathan snorted. "You might have been at one time, but you have no credibility with anyone now."

The short man at the end ignored him. "Yet in Christ we are all equal. We are all sinners, we are all in need of a Savior. And all I brag about anymore is that He forgave me and paid the price for my salvation."

"Amen!" several chorused.

"That's all any of us in this room can be proud of," James echoed.

A number nodded in agreement.

"I denied Him," Peter said, shaking his head.

"All of us have been forgiven for much," James responded. "And while you denied him and while Paul, here, persecuted His followers, the rest of the apostles ran away during His hour of need. And I did not understand Him while He was among us. Yet all of us have been forgiven. There is no upper or lower class in this group."

"Bah!" snorted one man at the end of the table. "Next thing they'll be having us treating women and slaves as equals."

"H'mm," the bald man sitting two places away from him, but close enough for Jonathan to hear, said. "In Christ there is neither East nor West, Jew nor Greek, slave nor free, male nor female. I like that."

Jonathan smiled. The arguing continued. He returned with another refilled pitcher.

"If the Lord thought enough of the Gentile believers to send His Holy Spirit to them and fill them just as He did us," someone commented, "who are we to say that they have not done enough to be saved?"

The bald man near Jonathan leaned toward the individual next to him. "I wrote an explanation of all of this to those Barnabas and I baptized in Galatia. Now I wish I'd brought a copy of it with me. It was all about adding burdens and rules after they had received their freedom through Jesus' blood. That epistle would be really helpful here."

"Perhaps," shrugged the man sitting next to him. "But I think they'd still argue."

"You're probably right."

As I stood watching with several other recording angels I shook my head. How patient the Creator is with human beings! His followers seem forever to be fighting over rules, even about good things. But what really matters is how God's people choose to handle such conflicts.

The discussions went on and on. Jonathan found his mind wandering and his arms aching from carrying the heavy jugs up and down the stairs as he kept refilling cups and food trays.

"Brothers," James said finally, "we have had much discussion here. We now need to go through the list of the important points and decide which we are going to include as we teach new believers. Above all, we need to keep it simple. There are the basic commandments that Yeshua taught. Beyond that . . ."

Jonathan glanced around. "I wonder who the short, bald guy on the end who talks so much is," he mumbled to himself.

"That's Paul," a tall man next to him whispered.

"Oh, I didn't realize that I said anything out loud," Jonathan apologized.

The other man smiled. "It's getting late, and we're all pretty tired. My name is Titus. I'm a friend of Paul's."

"I'm Jonathan. My mother is Martha, who has had charge of all the food."

"Give her my compliments," Titus said.

"Is that *the* Paul, the one who used to persecute the church?"

"The very one."

"It disturbs many of us," continued one of the men in the circle, "that the Gentiles are used to eating animals that have been strangled. Everyone knows that animals should be properly butchered and have all the blood drained from them before they are fit to eat. Yet Gentiles actually catch the blood and use it in their cooking. No self-respecting Jew is going to be able to eat at the same table."

A murmur of agreement rippled around the room.

"In many of the places we have visited," another commented, "there seems to be a problem with sexual immorality. And while those who grew up as Jews have strict laws about this, some of our new converts have no guilt whatsoever about doing all kinds of things that we would find impure and sinful. We must teach them to keep themselves sexually pure."

Many strongly endorsed his suggestion.

Jonathan turned to Titus. "I've heard about things like that."

"Sadly, some of our believers, even after they have been baptized, still think it is all right to live the way that they used to. It is an important issue. I guess that's why we had this meeting."

Finally, after many hours, James called for the conclusion. The delegates voted, and James made the announcement.

"Brothers, we are not going to burden the new Gentile believers with the entire ritual law, even if Moses did give it to us. But we must request several things of them. First, we will teach them about sexual purity and to stay away from sexual immorality. Second, we will ask them not to worship idols or buy food already offered to idols, because many people regard that as a form of worship. Finally, we will tell them to not eat meat from animals that have been strangled and not to consume blood. I think we are agreed that these things are enough. And beyond this the Holy Spirit will lead each person if there are more things in their lives the Lord wishes them to change."

The meeting concluded. Although Jonathan was exhausted, he and his stepmother still had a lot of cleaning up to do.

The delegates broke into several little knots of believers that continued to discuss things among themselves. A few left angry. Jonathan wondered if they would accept the decision of the group or if they would make trouble later.

I didn't wonder at all. I knew we would hear more from them as they tried to undermine the leadership of the new Christian church.

ELIHU BEN MALCHUS

elp! Help me!" Malchus screamed. "Somebody help!"

Elihu sprang to his father's sleeping mat. "Wake up, wake up! You're having another nightmare."

"No! No! It's real," he shouted. "Yeshua of Nazareth—He's got a sword."

The son put his arms around his father. "Wake up, Abba. Nobody's going to hurt you."

Dripping with cold perspiration and shaking, Malchus opened his eyes. "There's no one here?" he asked.

"No one but me."

"Where's your mother?"

"She's serving late in the house of the high priest. Remember they had a big feast tonight."

"Oh. Where is Yeshua?"

"Abba, don't you remember? Yeshua was crucified. It was a long time ago. I was just a little boy then."

The man shook his head. "I could have sworn He was in here. He had a sword and was going to hurt me like last time."

"It wasn't Yeshua that hurt you. One of His servants cut your ear off and Yeshua picked it up and put it back on. Yeshua cared about you. He healed you even though you were part of the party that arrested Him."

"Oh, yes," the older man mumbled. "He put my ear back." He reached up and felt it. "It's still there."

Elihu laughed shakily. "Yes, apparently He put it on pretty well."

"It would be easy to become one of His followers," Malchus said.

A look of pain crossed Elihu's face, although in the darkness I was the only one who could see it.

"Really?" he asked. "Really, Abba? If it would be that easy, why don't you become one?"

Hugging himself, Malchus started to rock back and forth in the dark and moan softly. "I can't, I just can't. Oh, it's so hard. You don't understand."

"Then tell me," his son said gently.

Malchus continued to rock. "I have such an important position. It—it just wouldn't be right. I owe some loyalty to the family of the high priest. I've been their servant all my life. I have an important position, you know," he repeated.

I watched the look of pain get deeper on Elihu's face. The father did once have an important position. But the high priest had told Elihu that Malchus had an evil spirit and that he was going insane. The religious leaders ordered the son to keep him out of their sight or his family would all be thrown out into the streets.

So far it had worked out well. Malchus did only the most menial tasks on the days when he was capable of doing anything other than rocking and mumbling to himself in the house. Elihu and his mother still served the priestly family and were able to keep their rooms in the servants' quarters.

"Abba," Elihu said with his arms around him, "you would be so much happier if you would just pick one or the other. This indecision is killing you and destroying your mind."

"Oh, you just don't understand," his father protested. "Nobody understands me. I have such an important position. There are so many issues. You don't know—you're just young."

Elihu took a deep breath. "Have a drink of water, Father. Maybe that will help you go back to sleep. And I have to lie back down now. I must leave early in the morning."

"Yes, yes, you must get your rest. I must get mine too. I—I have an important position, you know."

"Yes, I know. Let's both get our sleep."

Morning found Elihu out before dawn. He made eye contact with a man near the Temple gate and followed him down into a little back street.

"There are big plans for Passover," Elihu whispered to him as soon as they paused in a dark corner. "They are going to arrest James."

"We've moved him to a new spot. He's hiding at . . ."

"Stop—don't tell me. If I'm questioned and I don't know, I cannot betray his hiding place. Just make sure he is well hidden and protected."

The other man nodded, and Elihu returned to the Temple.

Passover was the busiest time of the year, and he as well as the Temple staff had many things to do. Glancing around, he decided that no one had followed him. Hopefully nobody had been watching from the rooftops, either. He shrugged. Sometimes he just had to trust that Yeshua would send a few extra angels to protect him. Working in the house of the high priest was a dangerous place for a follower of the Way.

Elihu ben Malchus hurried up the steps of the Temple. It was not even light yet, but he needed an early start. Passover was such a busy time, and there were so many things to do to prepare for it. He was no longer the wiry little boy he had been at the time Yeshua of Nazareth taught in the Temple courtyard. Now he was the tallest of the high priest's servants and the stockiest. As he smiled wryly he wondered if it was more of a curse than a blessing. It seemed the more his father shrunk into the frightened little man he had become, the more Elihu had grown and the more advantage the high priest took of it.

Shaking his head, he tried to dispel the morbid thoughts. *Now, Elihu,* he said to himself, *stop that! You gave your life to Yeshua of Nazareth. You pray and ask His Father to guide you every day just as He did, and if He still wants you to work here in the Temple, then you must do so until He guides you elsewhere.* Elihu wrinkled his nose at the stench of burning sacrifices. While he would work here today, he didn't have to enjoy it.

He stood in his position on the steps as the sheep merchants arrived to set up their booths beside the moneychangers. How Elihu despised all of them. As light broke over the horizon he stepped down from the steps to the first animal booth.

"What?" its owner demanded crossly.

"You know what," Elihu replied with a sigh. "We go through this every year."

"I paid my Temple taxes," the man protested.

"Yes, you did, and now you need to pay rent for your booth and a percentage of the sheep for the priests."

"There's nothing about this in the law of Moses."

Elihu laughed bitterly. "No, this is the law of Caiaphas, but you still have to pay."

Grumbling, the merchant passed over the required coinage.

"Now remember," Elihu added, "you also need to pay 10 percent of the switchovers."

As he went to the next booth Elihu shook his head and sighed. That practice particularly disgusted him. The switchovers were the sheep that the priests rejected as not good enough to sacrifice to God. The weary pilgrims would go back out to buy a perfect lamb from the vendors since they had to have a sacrifice. The sheep merchants would offer them a low price for their imperfect animals, but at least it would help toward the price of an acceptable one. As soon as the worshiper had left, the vendor would put the rejected lamb in with the rest of the stock, since usually there was nothing wrong with them anyway. These animals were considered switchovers and were how the animal vendors made extra profit during Passover.

Elihu hated that honest worshipers would get cheated. Even more, he detested the fact that the high priest, who was supported by the Temple taxes and the sacrifices outlined in the law, would cheat honest worshipers and be a part of such a scheme. *How offensive it must be to God,* he thought, then smiled grimly as he remembered Yeshua throwing everyone out of the courtyard. "How I miss Him!" he mumbled.

"You said something?" the next sheep vendor asked him.

"No," Elihu said quickly. "Nothing. Do you have your payment ready?"

"What are you going to do if I don't?" the man snarled. "Beat me up?"

Elihu took a deep breath. "No. I'm physically able, but I don't beat people up. You see those men over there?" He pointed to the elite Temple guard.

The man nodded nervously.

"They would thrash you. Why don't you just pay it, because there's nothing we can do about it."

The sheep farmer looked suspiciously at Elihu and passed over the money.

Elihu was not even halfway through the courtyard when a huge scuffle broke out behind him. The knot of angry and shouting people burst its way through the entry and up the steps and into the courtyard. The Temple guard rushed down. Elihu turned and walked over. One of the priests had run down the steps with undue haste. "Have you got him?" he asked.

"Right here," someone in the mob yelled back. The men parted, revealing a badly beaten man lying on the ground.

The guard poked him with the end of his staff. "Stand up."

The man struggled to his feet. One of his arms hung at an awkward angle, and he picked it up by his limp wrist and held it close to him.

"That's obviously broken," Elihu said, staring at the arm. Suddenly recognition flashed into his mind. This wasn't just anyone. The victim of the mob was James. James the believer. James the brother of John and one of the best friends of Yeshua of Nazareth.

Elihu felt as if his stomach had dropped down into his feet. What could he do? He drew closer.

"Excellent," the priest told the mob. He turned to James, "I can't tell you how pleased we are to see you."

For a moment Elihu made eye contact with James. The leader of the Way shook his head almost imperceptibly, but enough that Elihu knew he was telling him not to intervene. Elihu walked as casually as he could up the steps to Caiaphas.

"What are you going to do with this man?" he asked.

The high priest laughed gleefully. "It's a little present to Annas. Don't say I can't pick out just the perfect gift for an occasion as important as the Passover."

Elihu tried to smile. "A member of the Way, I suppose?"

"Yes," Caiaphas said. "He's one of the three main leaders. Don't you recognize him?"

After glancing at the battered James, Elihu replied, "It's hard to recognize a face that isn't there anymore."

"Ah, how true. I'm going to send him over to Herod. The Romans are useless for this kind of thing, but I think we can get what we want from him."

"Probably so."

"Well," Caiaphas continued, "we can't stand around here chatting all day. You have fees to collect."

"Yes, I guess I should get back to that."

With a heavy heart he walked back down the steps. He had to keep working. Caiaphas was watching him. What else could he do? How could he save James? God, show me what to do, he cried inside of himself as he tried to keep his face emotionless. Show me what to do. But the leaden skies were silent.

Since Elihu was not Temple staff but in the personal service of Caiaphas, his job was wherever the high priest was and whatever he was told to do. He stood in the background as Caiaphas entertained dignitaries at dinner. Passover was a time when people came from all over the world to Jerusalem to worship. And it was a time for the finest dining and entertaining in all of the wealthy homes. The priests were no exception.

Suddenly a messenger slipped in and, apologizing, whispered something in the ear of Caiaphas. The high priest's face turned dark red and then purple. "Why did he do that?" he exploded. "How dare he ruin all my plans!"

Elihu stepped forward, anticipating immediate orders, but none came.

Caiaphas continued to shout. "I had him arrested so that we could have a public execution and make a point. What is wrong with that little weasel Herod? How can he be afraid of these uneducated little peasants? Why do the Romans even let him rule?"

Immediately a little knot of priests formed at the head of the table and soon Caiaphas quieted down. He gave a few apologies and excused himself from the dinner.

As soon as he could Elihu slipped into the kitchen where his mother was working. "Have you heard?" he asked her.

She nodded, not looking up from her work.

"I wanted to help," her son mumbled. "Now it's too late."

His mother reached out and rubbed his shoulder. "Elihu, there's only one Savior."

Tears rolled down his cheeks in spite of himself. "It just seems that because I'm working here I could have done something."

His mother looked him in the eye. "You stay alive," she said. "Your time will come when He will need you. But you stay here until He tells you—and stay alive."

Brushing his tears away, he once again hid behind his emotionless expression. "We need more meat in the other room. They've almost finished those platters."

"I'll see to it immediately. Now check on your father."

* * *

When Elihu walked into the kitchens the excitement in the air was almost palpable. He reported to the head steward.

"Today you need to stick near Caiaphas in case he needs you for personal errands. They arrested that big fisherman, one of the leaders of the Way. Our master is in a much better mood today. He will discuss the details of a public execution with Herod. Hopefully there will still be time left during the Passover celebration."

His face completely impassive, Elihu nodded.

"For now have some breakfast," the steward continued. "The high priest is up, but he's having a private meeting in his chambers with Annas and some of the other priests. As soon as they're done I imagine you'll be gone all day."

When Elihu sat down and tried to eat, everything stuck in his throat. Now they had Peter too. He closed his eyes tight. *Yeshua, are You seeing this? Are You watching? Are You going to do anything?*

Silently Elihu waited as Caiaphas paced back and forth in front of the prisoner. "Well," he said, "we've got you now. We killed James, and your precious Yeshua did nothing about it. That's because He's dead." The high priest spat the word "dead" as if it tasted bad.

"Yes," Peter said, "you've killed James. It was an honor for him to serve Yeshua of Nazareth, Son of God. And it was an honor for James to die for Him too. My fellow leader was completely devoted to Him."

"Well," the high priest snapped, "with any luck we'll be able to honor you in the same way this weekend. Only we're hoping for a public execution this time."

Peter met him with a level gaze. "Your plans with James didn't completely work out?"

"Silence!" the religious leader shouted. "You will speak only when spoken to."

"I take my orders from Yeshua of Nazareth," Peter replied gently. "If you've been able to arrest me, it's because He has allowed it. And if He allows you to put me to death, then that's His will too. But if He is not willing to allow it now, there's nothing you'll be able to do about it. I'm content to wait and see what His intent is for me."

"Get him out of here," Caiaphas shrieked. He turned to Herod. "You've been unusually quiet."

"Oh," Herod replied abstractedly. "I was just listening. Um— guards, place him in the dungeon. Rotate four squads with him. Chain two guards to each wrist; then we'll see what this Yeshua can do for him."

Peter smiled. "Four squads! I rate 16 soldiers? It seems you respect Yeshua and His power too."

"Come on," a guard ordered, yanking Peter by the chains on his wrist. "Let's get you to the dungeon before you make them so angry that they execute you in the great hall."

Elihu drew a deep breath. *Yeshua, are You watching?* he whispered inside his head. *Are You seeing this? Do You have a plan?*

I smiled. There was always a plan. Humans just couldn't always see what it was. The fact that sometimes followers of Yeshua die discourages them and they forget that there is still a master plan, and that while the enemy takes temporary prisoners, it does not change the outcome of the battle. I wanted to scoop him up in my arms and whisper that everything was going to be fine, but I stood as I was supposed to and proudly watched my charge standing as he was supposed to, although with less confidence than I.

The rest of the day Elihu kept busy delivering messages from the priests back and forth to various members of the Sanhedrin and to Herod.

"This is your last one," Caiaphas said, handing him a scroll that the scribe had just sealed. "You've had a long day."

"Thank you," Elihu said. His stomach had been in a knot all day as he had heard the plans for a public execution of the fisherman. He had been wracking his brains, yet could come up with nothing that could save Peter now. Who could help him in a dungeon? And even if he could get in, the guards would outnumber him. Sixteen men assigned to watch one man. He shook his head. "I guess the only thing I can do is pray about it," he mumbled.

I almost laughed. Why do humans think that their actions are so important and resort to prayer only as a last effort, when their prayers are the most powerful help they could employ? Perhaps he would learn as he got older.

Darting into an alley, he watched carefully to see if anyone had followed him. When he was certain that no one was paying him any attention, he turned the other direction and headed for the house with the large upper room. He had heard that many in the Way were up there praying for Peter's release. Since he could think of nothing else to do, he decided to join them.

Knocking on the door, he gave the secret password. "Have you any news of Peter?" Rhoda, the young servant minding the door, asked him.

"None. I've just come from the home of Caiaphas. Peter is still in the dungeon. The execution is planned for tomorrow."

She burst into tears. "Come this way," she said finally. "Everyone is upstairs."

Although believers crowded the room, it was very quiet except for the whisper of prayers. Fear had snaked its tentacles through the room and seemed to have a good grasp on everyone. Not knowing what else to do, he just stood with the others and began to pray too. Hours passed, but no one was hungry and no one wanted to leave. Elihu was glad he had told his mother not to worry about him tonight. It looked as if they would be there all night.

Later Elihu was not sure how much time had passed, but it seemed as if it would be morning before long. All of the believers were still huddled together and still praying quietly among themselves. Everyone was nervous and jumped at the slightest sound.

Suddenly they heard a pounding on the door downstairs. Everyone froze. Accusing eyes turned to Elihu. "Have you betrayed us too?" asked one believer. "No wonder they knew where to come for Peter and James."

"No, no, I didn't," he protested. "I'm a believer too."

"Aren't you a servant of Caiaphas?"

Elihu gulped and nodded. "Yes, it's true. I have not known what else to do so far."

"Right," someone muttered.

John Mark's mother, the owner of the home, strode over and put her hand on Rhoda's shoulder. "Please answer the door. It does not do to keep them waiting, whether they are friends or enemies come to arrest us. And you," she turned to Elihu's accusers, "leave him alone. It's best not to make accusations unless you know for sure."

"Well, it's obvious, isn't it?" one person countered.

"Maybe." Then linking her arm through Elihu's, she said, "Come over here by the fire." She led him to the small coal brazier set up in the center of the room to ward off the night chill. "Stay away from them," she said. "They're just scared, and when people's fright exceeds their faith, they can get a little nasty."

He smiled weakly. Since it had never occurred to him that the believers would be afraid of him or view him as a spy, he didn't know what to say.

Suddenly Rhoda's feet pounded up the stairs and she burst into the room. "It's Peter! It's Peter. I can't believe it." She was laughing and crying at once. "It's Peter! It really is!"

"Right!" said the man who had been accusing Elihu moments before. "Your fear has made you start seeing things."

"Maybe she's not crazy," another person suggested. "Maybe they've executed him, too, and this is his angel in his form come to let us know his fate."

"Did you open the door?" John Mark's mother asked the girl.

"Uh—no, I was so surprised that it's really Peter!"

The woman shook her head. "Rhoda, go back down. Open the door. Bring him in. If it really is Peter, it hardly does to let him stand out in the street where he can get arrested again." The girl raced back down the stairs. Everyone stood motionless. Could it really be Peter?

Deciding to find out for himself, Elihu hurried down to the door. Several others followed him. He immediately recognized the person standing at the gate. When Peter saw them and everyone began asking questions all at once, he motioned for them to be quiet.

The others fell silent.

"I was chained to the wall in the dungeon," Peter began. "And I had two Romans chained to each side of me, so I really couldn't move at all without disturbing one of them, too."

"I'm sure they loved that," someone muttered as more crowded into the courtyard by the gate.

"They weren't happy about it. Since they had taken off my robes and my sandals, I was in just my undergarment, which was pretty chilly on that stone floor."

People nodded. Everyone had heard tales about what prisons were like.

"I was sleeping and so were they when suddenly an angel awakened me. I think he prodded me on the shoulder a couple times."

Several of the apostles burst out laughing. Barnabas turned to Elihu and said, "That's how you can tell it's a true story. Even an angel can't wake Peter up by just speaking to him. It's amazing those Romans got any sleep at all if Peter fell asleep first." The fisherman was known for his thunderous snoring.

"Do you want to hear my story or not?" Peter protested.

"Yes, yes, go on," Barnabas replied.

"The angel awakened me and told me to get dressed. Handed me my clothes and my sandals. The chains just fell off and the Romans never moved a whisker."

"All of them?" asked one believer.

"Everyone on guard duty. Sleeping more soundly than I ever have. Then the angel led me to the gate. It just fell open—he didn't even touch it. All the sentries at the gates were asleep too. I followed him clear out into the street, past the iron gate that leads into the city. It swung open and clanged shut behind us. And then he left me. So I came here."

"God be praised," someone said. And the room broke into praises and prayers.

"You see," Peter said, "we have no reason to be afraid. Some of us may die and some of us may be beaten, but it's not going to happen unless the Lord allows it. And when it does, He will give us the courage that we need to deal with it. And in the meantime, if He has other plans for us, all the schemes that the Romans and the priests make are worth nothing."

I smiled as I watched the celebrating humans. If only they could remember this all the time, how much anguish it would save them.

It was almost morning. The sky was getting lighter as the believers began to leave in little knots of two and three from the house so as not to be conspicuous.

Peter turned to Elihu. "You, young man," he said, "you are a servant of Caiaphas."

"Yes."

"I thought I recognized you. It is time for you to leave the house of the priest. You are in danger."

Elihu looked at the ground. "My father is ill, and my mother works for them too. They need me."

The women had stood to one side, for though the men and women of the Way mixed more freely than the Jews of Jerusalem did, they still were more comfortable in separate groups. A heavily veiled woman approached Peter. As she lifted her veil Elihu recognized her.

"Mother."

"It is time, my son," she said. "I have been praying about this for years, and I knew that the time would come."

"But what about Father—what about you? I can't leave you—you're in danger too."

"No, I don't believe that I am, and as long as your father lives, I will be there to care for him. He's my husband. But you are in danger, and the fisherman is right. We have been praying for years that Yeshua would let us know when the time was right. So now that He's telling us we must not ignore Him."

"But what am I going to do? Where should I go? Did He tell you that?"

"My son is going on a journey soon," the woman who had brought him over to the brazier said. "He's about your age."

"Where is he going?" Elihu's mother asked.

"I'm not sure, but he's going to travel with Barnabas whom your son met earlier here. And Saul."

"You mean the one who has persecuted the Way?" Elihu said in surprise.

"The very one." She smiled. "They want to share the word with Gentiles."

"I see," Elihu's mother said. "But do they have a definite plan yet?"

"Not that I know of," John Mark's mother replied.

"Well," Elihu's mother said after thinking a moment, "I have a sister who lives in Lystra."

"Lystra! That's a long way from Judea."

"Well, yes. She was kind of a disappointment to our family. It seems she married a Greek and moved there, although she still worships the God of Israel. My sister just—well, she married a Greek; what can I say? Anyway, they live in Lystra, and I believe they have a son about the same age as my son."

"Well," John Mark's mother said, "it's possible that they may plan their route through there and could take Elihu with them. He could stay in Lystra where he would be safe. The high priest has no influence there."

"The Lord is always able to work things out," Elihu's mother observed. "If He can get Peter out of jail with all those soldiers guarding him, I'm sure getting Elihu to Lystra is a small thing."

The women laughed. "Let's talk to them," they said.

By the next day Peter had left for Caesarea. Elihu had met Mark. His name was John Mark, but Elihu just called him Mark because he knew too many Johns. He had talked more with Barnabas, and they were making plans for the journey. But Elihu was sure the trip would go fine, and could hardly keep his mind on his duties while he waited for them to decide a definite time of departure.

Even Caiaphas noted his absentminded behavior and mentioned it after having to speak to him twice about a message to be delivered.

"I apologize," Elihu said. "I have not slept well the past few nights. My father, you know."

The high priest nodded. "Yes, I'm sure it must be difficult.

However, I need you to have your mind on your work here or you will be useless to me—as useless as your father has become," he muttered under his breath, but loud enough for Elihu to hear.

Although Elihu's face reddened, he said nothing. He hoped he could leave soon.

*　*　*

The guardians hovered near the boat about to depart on the Mediterranean journey, as they had on the land journey up to Seleucia in Syria.

Saul and the young John Mark lay below deck propped against the side of the boat doing their best to keep their stomachs stable. Tempers were short and became shorter as the two became more seasick. Barnabas remained below, trying to keep the two from arguing, and occasionally offering sips of water.

Elihu stayed up on deck. He would far rather take the stinging salt spray in his face than Saul's hostility toward Mark. He thought Caiaphas had been the most caustic person he'd ever met in his life, but apparently he was wrong.

His spirits lifted as the harbor of Salamis came into view. It was beautiful. "Is that it?" he asked one of the sailors. "Is this Cyprus?"

"Sure is," the sailor replied cheerfully. "The best harbor on the island, it has deep water, which makes it easy for even the largest ships to come in here. Because of that, all the finest copper, flax, wine, fruit, and honey are traded here and then exported to all the Mediterranean ports nearby."

"I wonder if there are any Jews here," Elihu mused to himself.

"There are," the sailor told him.

"I didn't realize I said that out loud," Elihu said, embarrassed.

"Oh, don't worry about it. Jews are always searching each other out. And there's a pretty good colony here. You'll probably be able to find friends that you knew in other places. We've taken a lot of

Jews to here from different ports, especially since some controversy a few years back. A person named Stephen got stoned, and people began fleeing Judea. It's kind of settled down a little now, but you never know when it might start up again."

Elihu nodded. He wondered what the sailor would say if he knew that Saul, who had been the ringleader of the persecution of the Way, was below deck. He decided this wasn't the time to mention that fact.

Upon leaving the ship, Barnabas and Elihu found lodging for their two seasick companions where they could clean up and rest until they recovered their land legs.

"Would you like to go look around Salamis while these two rest?" Barnabas asked. "I have some friends here."

Elihu broke into a wide grin. That sounded much better than waiting for their two companions to get over their seasickness and become friendly again.

I followed the two on their explorations. After all, I was recording Elihu's choices. The guardians could take care of the other two.

As they wandered through the market Elihu drank in the new sights and sounds and smells. "Cyprus is a beautiful place," he blurted out at one point.

Barnabas nodded. "Yes, but then I would think so because it's my home. My calling is in Antioch right now, but every time I get an opportunity I come back here."

"I can understand why," Elihu said.

"Over there is the citadel," Barnabas pointed.

Elihu glanced in that direction. "Who lives there?"

"The proconsul of the island. His name is Sergius Paulus."

"I wish we could see the inside of the palace," Elihu said wistfully.

Barnabas raised an eyebrow. "Well, I guess it depends on why one is inside the palace as to whether it would be much fun."

"What do you mean?"

"If you get invited there as a guest, it would be pretty marvelous, and you would probably enjoy it. But if the authorities dragged you in there because you were in trouble, it would not be much fun."

"Oh, I hadn't even thought about that. Do you think that Sergius Paulus will give us a hard time?"

"I don't know," Barnabas said. "He's always seemed to be a pretty reasonable man, but I don't think that they have had conflicts here with Christ's followers yet. We'll find out."

Elihu still wished he could see the inside of the palace, although the idea of appearing there as a prisoner sounded frightening.

Paul and the young John Mark were soon feeling better and began traveling all over the island preaching about Jesus.

One day the four of them had been walking for hours. As they crested a little hill a beachside village came into view. Barnabas took a deep, satisfied sigh and said, "It's Kition. My home."

"Really?" Elihu asked. "Do you have family there?"

"Some—and friends. And, if things have gone well, perhaps some friends from Jerusalem, too."

They hurried down the hill and approached a house. Barnabas knocked and called out, "It's Barnabas."

The door flung open, and much shouting and hugging followed as Barnabas greeted everyone. Then turning to his three companions, he said, "I have guests with me," and introduced them.

A tall man, who had been busily hugging Barnabas and slapping him on the back, turned pale, and his jaw clenched. "How can you bring this man into our home and put all of our lives in danger?" he demanded.

"Please, Lazarus, he's my guest," Barnabas whispered.

The man frowned and said nothing.

"Friends, this is my family," Barnabas said, gesturing toward the people clustered by the door. "This is my mother and my sister, Mary, and this is Lazarus of Bethany, who moved here with the other Marys for safety during—uh—the persecution in Jerusalem."

Saul silently looked at the ground while Lazarus' jaw clenched harder.

"This Mary is Jesus' mother," Barnabas continued. "And this Mary is Lazarus' sister. Around here if you just call Mary, one of them will come," he said with a smile.

Mark and Elihu laughed at his little joke, then stopped quickly, realizing that the three of them were the only ones to find it amusing. The others stood with stony expressions.

"This is Saul," Barnabas said, pointing to the little man. "He follows Christ now."

"So he says," Mary, the sister of Lazarus, hissed.

Saul raised his eyes to her. "How can you hold my life before Christ against me?"

"Enough!" Lazarus exploded. "Do you insult my sister in my own home?"

"Stop! Stop!" Barnabas said, waving his arms. "This is not how this was supposed to go. Jesus has changed all of our lives. None of us would have been friends a few years ago. But He has brought all of us together. He has forgiven and cleansed all of us. Saul has become a Christian and is a preacher of the good news about Christ. In His service he has traveled many places and suffered many things, and it is not fair to hold his past against him any more than it is fair to remember Mary's past. And Lazarus, my friend, you were once a dead body. How would you feel if our fellow Jews treated you as unclean because of that fact?"

Lazarus almost cracked a smile. "I hadn't thought of that."

Small smiles teased at the corners of several mouths, and the group became less tense.

"Let's start this over," Barnabas said after a moment. "My family, meet my friends. And my friends, meet my family. We are one in Christ. Now, can we do this without fighting with each other?"

Lazarus bowed. "Friends of Barnabas and friends of Christ are welcome in my home. Please come in."

Elihu enjoyed the days they spent in Kition. Lazarus and the various Marys were hungry for news of Jerusalem.

"How's my sister?" Mary, the sister of Lazarus, inquired one day. "Is she and her family well?"

"Yes," Barnabas said. "And they still live in your family home in Bethany. They have provided shelter and comfort for many Christians fleeing Jerusalem, and so far they have escaped the persecution."

"And do they have children? I know that when my sister married Doud he had that young redheaded son of his."

Barnabas laughed. "Well, now they have several running around. And your sister is very happy. She does all the organizing of any of our get-togethers there."

"Yes, she's the most organized person I know. I feel that when the gifts were given to us at birth, she got enough domestic gifts for the both of us, and so I didn't receive any."

"What about John?" asked Mary, Jesus' mother.

"He is well," Barnabas answered, smiling at her. "He sends his love, and as soon as he feels it is safe, he will come back for you and bring you to the family home."

The catching up went on and on. Saul remained uncharacteristically quiet unless someone asked him a specific question. Mary, Jesus' mother, headed to where Elihu and Mark sat.

"You two look homesick," she said. "Tell me about your families."

Mark smiled. "I don't think we've met before, but my mother owns the home where your Son the Christ rented the room to celebrate Passover right before—before—well, you know."

"That's wonderful. I knew your mother well. She's a sweet woman. I'm sure she really misses you."

His eyes glistened, and she tactfully turned to Elihu. "What about your family, Elihu? Are you from Jerusalem too?"

"I am. My father and mother both work for Caiaphas, but my mother and I are followers of the Christ, though my mother has to do that secretly."

"And you father—does he believe in my Son?"

Elihu frowned. "He can't make up his mind, and it has made him unwell. He was in the garden that night when Peter rushed up and tried to behead him with the sword. My father ducked just in time and had only his ear slashed off. Yeshua picked up Father's ear from the ground and put it right back on his head and it was as if it had never been wounded, except there was blood all over the place so we could tell it had been. His ear has been fine since then, but his mind has not. I feel that if he decided one way or the other, he would be better off. But feeling torn and refusing to make a decision is destroying him."

"It's true," Mary said with a sigh. "Indecision can be more destructive than a wrong choice sometimes. So how did you come to be with the group here?"

"It was dangerous for followers of the Christ in the house of Caiaphas. My mother is sending me with Saul and Barnabas, hoping that in their travels they will go to Lystra. I have an aunt there. She's married to a Greek, so the family has been estranged from her for many years, but now her home seems to be a safe place to send me. I wanted to stay and help care for my father and protect my mother, but she insisted that I go."

Mary nodded. "You are a good and obedient son. And I believe God will bless you for honoring your mother and obeying her even when all your own instincts make you want to stay. God will care for her even more effectively than you could." She smiled. "He honors the obedience of His followers."

Both young men leaned against the wall and stared up at the star-dusted sky. Talking to Mary had made them miss their own families even more.

It was late in the night when the visiting finished and the fire burned down to glowing coals.

* * *

The two young men leaned against a tree a short distance from where Saul was loudly preaching about Jesus. They had heard his sermons so many times that their minds were wandering this afternoon. Elihu was drawing in the sand with a stick.

"What is it?" Mark asked when he noticed what the other was doing.

"Oh, it's a self-portrait."

As he stared at it Mark started laughing. "Doesn't look like anything that I recognize. Here, let me try."

A few moments later Mark stood up. Elihu studied it. "What is that? Are you saying I'm a donkey?"

"Sure. You're the beast of burden. They make you carry everything."

Elihu laughed. "Well, that's because you're the scribe, so you're supposed to be writing down everything that they say."

Mark's smile slowly faded from his face.

"Well, what's the matter? Aren't you recording what they preach? I see you writing all the time."

"Yes, I—I am writing all the time."

"Well, you write. I carry things. Saul preaches."

"What about Barnabas?"

"He's the fireman," Elihu said.

"Fireman? What do you mean? You're the one who always starts the fires in the evening."

Elihu laughed. "Those are just the cooking fires. Your cousin Barnabas stamps out all the fires that Saul starts by the way some people react to him. Think about it. Everywhere Saul has gone eventually he's gotten thrown out of the place. Now he's with your cousin Barnabas, and Barnabas soothes over everyone's feelings and keeps him from starting big arguments. He hasn't been beaten or thrown out of any place since we've been here. Although it almost happened in Kition."

They grinned at each other.

"You're right," Mark said. "Perhaps God put my uncle and Saul together because Saul needed to learn some diplomatic skills and maybe my uncle will become a little more assertive. He's terribly shy."

"It could be," Elihu mused. "My mother has often said that everyone in our life is there for a reason. That even if they are really annoying, there is something we can learn from them and that we should thank God for them and treat them as though He put them there on purpose, instead of being upset at them. But it never made any sense to me until now."

Mark stared at the ground. "You're a—you're a better person than I am, Elihu."

"What do you mean? We're all pretty equal now. The Christ died for both of us, and we both needed a Savior. We were both sinners."

"Oh, it's not that. I just—I don't want to be part of this group anymore. I just want to go home. I know that there are things I could learn from Saul. And I know he is a great preacher. My uncle says he is the greatest preacher in the Christian movement right now. But we just don't get along. I think he *really* doesn't like me. So I just want to go home."

"At least you can go home," Elihu said with a smile. "My life would have been in danger if I had remained in Jerusalem. I had to come. And I don't think I can go home for a long time."

Both looked at each other for a long moment. Then they both turned their attention back to the preaching, and nothing more was said.

* * *

Another day. Another town.

"Hey, we have our own son of Jesus here," someone shouted at Paul from the crowd.

"Yes. Elymas bar Jesus," others echoed.

"But Jesus of Nazareth," Saul protested, "was the Son of God. He could do miracles. Jesus healed the sick and even raised the dead."

"Well, our son of Jesus can do all kinds of miracles too," a townsperson exclaimed. "You need to meet him. He's powerful."

"But Jesus of Nazareth—" Saul continued.

The crowd shouted him down. "Get Elymas! Get Elymas bar Jesus! Let him meet our son of Jesus."

By now no one could hear Saul. The crowd started chanting, "Elymas! Elymas! Elymas!"

Soon an entourage approached the crowd. It was Elymas. As he neared Saul, someone shouted out, "Preacher of Jesus of Nazareth, meet Elymas, son of Jesus."

The evangelist nodded to the man. Elymas put his hand out, and suddenly gold coins appeared in it. He threw them to the cheering crowd.

"It's your turn, Saul. What can you do?" they shouted. "What kind of power did Jesus of Nazareth give you?"

Saul remained silent.

Reaching toward the evangelist, Elymas seemed to pull some small sweet cakes from behind the preacher's shoulder. "That's an unusual place to keep your lunch," he said. The crowd roared, and he tossed the treats to the crowd.

"This man is just a showman," Saul proclaimed. "A magician. Jesus of Nazareth is a God."

"Elymas is our prophet," someone said from the crowd.

"He's no prophet," Saul retorted. "He's a cheap magician."

A brawl appeared about to break out. Soldiers appeared on the periphery. "What's the problem here?" demanded the officer in charge.

"It's a contest of powers," someone explained.

"Yes, between Jesus of Nazareth and Elymas bar Jesus," another added.

"No, it's not Jesus of Nazareth. It's this Saul person," a third individual interrupted.

"Well, save it for the proconsul," the officer said. "He wants to meet this Saul person anyway. As one of his advisers, you know he's fond of you, Elymas. Let's all head back to the palace where we can settle this in a civilized way."

"Fine with me," Elymas agreed. He turned to Saul. "I am at the palace frequently. Have you ever been there?"

Saul looked like a thundercloud. Elihu's stomach twisted into a knot. Now he was going to see the inside of the palace. But was it a good thing? He wasn't sure.

When at the palace Saul received permission to speak he started to tell the story of Jesus of Nazareth to the proconsul. Over on the side Elymas kept making comments that the little evangelist could not quite hear, but that made everyone around the magician laugh.

Suddenly Saul turned to him and said, "You work for the devil. Every night you stay up inventing schemes to cheat people out of God, but now you've come up against Him yourself. And for that you're about to go blind for a while, unable to see even the sun."

Elymas smiled and said, "Hah!" but it ended in a high-pitched squeak, and suddenly his hands shot out. "Help me!" he cried. "Help me. I can't see. Something's happened. I can't see."

While Elymas' friends clustered around him to sooth his panic, Saul waited patiently. "Why don't you lead him to someplace where he can sit down? He may want to hear this," he said after a few minutes.

Then Saul gave his complete sermon uninterrupted. The proconsul appeared impressed.

So were Mark and Elihu. Afterward they asked him, "How did

you do that, Saul?"

"I didn't. I was just praying and asking God what I should do. And He told me."

"That's great!" Elihu said.

Mark just looked sick.

"So how's the writing coming?" Saul asked him, trying to change the subject. "I've seen you scratching away there, and you've filled up one or two scrolls. Why don't you read some of it to us?"

"Oh, I—I don't want to do that," Mark stammered.

"Oh, come on," Barnabas insisted. "We want to hear what you've written. You've been listening to all Saul's sermons. By now you must have many of them recorded."

"I—um—this really isn't a good time," the young man stammered.

"Nonsense, boy. Get them out. Let's see what you've got."

"I'm not feeling very well," he mumbled. But he unrolled one of his scrolls and began to read. "'The good news of Jesus Christ—the Message—begins here, following to the letter the scroll of the prophet Isaiah.

"Watch closely: I'm sending my preacher ahead of you;
He'll make the road smooth for you.
Thunder in the desert!
Prepare for God's arrival!
Make the road smooth and straight!"'" (Mark 1:1-3, Message).

"Did I quote that passage from Isaiah?" Saul asked, puzzled.

"Go on," Barnabas urged.

"'John the Baptizer appeared in the wild, preaching a baptism of life-change that leads to forgiveness of sins. People thronged to him from Judea and Jerusalem and, as they confessed their sins, were baptized by him in the Jordan River into a changed life. John wore a camel-hair habit, tied at the waist with a leather belt. He ate locusts and wild field honey'" (verses 4-6, Message).

"I never said that," Saul frowned.

Mark stopped.

"Continue," Barnabas said.

"But that's nothing like what I have been preaching." Saul shook his head, a confused expression on his face.

"Keep reading," Barnabas insisted.

"Are you sure?" Mark asked nervously.

"Yes, keep reading."

"'As he preached he said, "The real action comes next: The star in this drama, to whom I'm a mere stagehand, will change your life. I'm baptizing you here in the river, turning your old life in for a kingdom life. His baptism—a holy baptism by the Holy Spirit—will change you from the inside out."

"'At this time, Jesus came from Nazareth in Galilee and was baptized by John in the Jordan. The moment he came out of the water, he saw the sky split open and God's Spirit, looking like a dove, come down on him. Along with the Spirit, a voice: "You are my Son, chosen and marked by my love, pride of my life"'" (verses 7-11, Message).

"But I have never told that story. That's not in any of my sermons," Saul protested.

Barnabas turned to Saul. "No," he said, "but it is the story of Jesus of Nazareth. Isn't that what you wanted?"

"Well—you said that your nephew was a scribe and that he could write down some of my sermons and we could circulate them among the new converts. And this is not what we discussed."

"No, it is not what we discussed. Mark?"

"I—I just wanted to write the story of Jesus. Your sermons are good, but they're all theology and history and why the Jews did this and the Jews did that. And why Jesus was the Messiah. By the time they're converts they want to hear more about Jesus, not more of what they've already heard."

As Saul jumped to his feet Barnabas stood too. "Now let's think about this," Mark's uncle said. "This—this could work. It could make good sense. After all, many people were with Jesus and knew Him and saw Him do a lot of things. It would be helpful to have a record of those stories. You—you might enjoy reading them."

"But it's *not* what we discussed," Saul replied. "Your nephew hasn't done anything the way he was supposed to on this whole journey. He's young, afraid, and can't take our pace. I was looking for an assistant and a personal scribe, and this is *not* what I expected it to be."

"No, it's not," Mark said. "None of it is what we discussed. And I'm not any happier than you are." He took a deep breath, shook his head, and said, "I'm not cut out for this kind of traveling life. I don't want to be your personal scribe. I just want to write the stories of Jesus the way they happened."

"This is totally unacceptable." Saul started pacing back and forth. "Totally unacceptable."

"I'm sure we can work this out," Barnabas replied, trying to soothe the upset evangelist. "You are one of the greatest preachers in our whole movement. But Mark's idea has value too, and there is—there is a place for that."

"There may be a place for both of us," Saul said after some moments, "but I don't think it's together."

Mark shook his head. "No, not together."

Barnabas sighed and thought for several minutes. "Suppose I arrange passage for you back to Israel, Mark? Can you get back to Jerusalem on your own?"

The younger man nodded.

"We're almost to Pamphylia. There's a harbor there. I will find a ship for your trip. Please continue your writing. It is something that we need. And no one has put the story of Jesus into writing."

"Perhaps there would be value someday in putting some of my words into writing," Saul muttered.

Barnabas turned to him. "Yes. We will find you a scribe who will take down your words and send them to encourage the converts in the places we have been. Even when the Lord was here, He used many different types of people, and we didn't all get along either. So this shouldn't be shocking or feel like a failure to anyone. It's just the Lord's way, and we need to learn to work with it. This will probably not be the first time that people He has called to ministry disagree and have trouble getting along."

I laughed out loud. God's people have always had conflicts with each other and have always had trouble getting along. Barnabas was quite correct. It always seemed to me that my job would be easier if God had more followers like Barnabas and fewer like Saul and Mark. However, if there were, the work would not get done in the same way, for after all, the Lord made special use of both Saul and young Mark. He has great patience with humans.

The rest of the trip to the port was tense. Barnabas, true to his word, bought Mark passage on a ship bound for Joppa. From there the young man would travel home to Jerusalem on his own.

After bidding him goodbye, the other three boarded another ship bound for Perga. From there they headed up to Pisidian, Antioch, Iconium, Lystra, and Derbe. It was a rough trip. Saul began to request that people now call him Paul.

"I'd like to take the name Paul," he said, "in honor of the governor, Sergius Paulus, who was very fair to us."

"Yes, he was," Elihu responded. "I wonder whatever happened to Elymas bar Jesus?"

"I don't know, but from now please address me as Paul. Perhaps that will help me get away from the image of a persecutor, and more people will just listen to my message instead of worrying about what I used to be."

Barnabas smiled. "The Lord has forgiven everything you used to be. But if you would rather be called Paul, we would be happy to oblige you."

The apostle launched into his preaching with new vigor in the town of Iconium. Soon the Jews in that town became furious and forced them to leave. While it was frightening, at least the missionaries encountered only the threat of violence. "Couldn't you be more cautious, Paul?" Elihu asked one day.

"More cautious?" he replied incredulously.

"Well, not that you would water down the gospel or change anything that Jesus of Nazareth said, but you just make people so angry."

"I can't help it if they're angry at what I say. They got angry at Jesus, too."

Elihu looked at Barnabas, who shrugged.

"Some people will always be angry when someone presents truth to them," Barnabas said. "Although there is a place for gentleness and diplomacy."

"I just preach it as it is," Paul muttered, pacing back and forth. "I just preach it as it is."

"That's true," Barnabas acknowledged.

"And many people have accepted the gospel," Paul protested.

"And that's also true. But perhaps there's a way to preach it without making people want to attack you."

"Perhaps," Paul said slowly. "I—I speak from the bottom of my heart. I mean every word I speak. But perhaps the two of us together . . ." He looked at Barnabas imploringly.

"Yes, that's why the two of us are together. We'll preach together at Lystra, the next village along that road. Perhaps team preaching together will work better."

"I certainly hope so," Elihu whispered under his breath, "because this is getting scary."

As they approached the town of Lystra, they noticed a crippled man sitting by the gate. He heard Paul talking and looked at him. The evangelist walked over to him. Suddenly Paul said in a loud voice, "Stand up on your feet." At the same time he pulled the man to his feet. To his amazement, the crippled man stood. Even when Paul let go he kept his balance. Then he took one tentative step and still another. Suddenly he began jumping and laughing and shouting.

"I can walk! I can walk! I've never been able to do this. Not since the day I was born. Praise the gods! This is wonderful!"

People came streaming out of houses and the market to see what had happened. They all started shouting and chanting, "Praise the gods! The gods have come down! Praise the gods!"

Because they were shouting in their own dialect, Paul and Barnabas were not exactly sure what the people were saying, so they smiled and nodded.

"It must be Zeus and Hermes come down. Zeus must be the tall good-looking one and Hermes the one who talks a lot. He must be his speaker," they said, pointing at Paul. "Get the priest from the temple of Zeus quick. Bring a bull. We must have a sacrifice immediately."

The people continued to cheer. It seemed only a few minutes until the priest from the local shrine had assembled a parade. It consisted of banners and bulls and people dancing and shouting and getting ready for a sacrifice.

"What are you doing?" Paul protested as he began to realize what was going on. "Stop this. No—don't sacrifice a bull to us. And don't worship us. We are not gods."

"No, no," Barnabas added. "I am not Zeus. Nor is he Hermes."

But the people didn't understand.

Elihu wished his friend Mark were there. Having gotten separated from Paul and Barnabas in the crowd, he glanced around frantically. This was Lystra—the town where his aunt should be. How would he ever find her in the huge crowd among all the pandemonium?

Suddenly he noticed some men he had seen in Iconium. They went straight to the priest of Zeus and whispered to him, then the city elders. Instantly the mood turned ugly. "They're impostors—they're not gods at all," the priest roared. "Stone them!"

Then the same people who had moments before shouted praises to those they thought were gods were now angry. The crowd surrounded Paul and Barnabas.

"Stop! Stop!" Elihu screamed. He threw himself against the mob, trying to get through to see what was happening, but he couldn't. Little did he know that the people he struggled against were guardians stationed all around him so that he would not be injured in the melee. Finally he gave up and sat sobbing on the stone steps of the acropolis.

Unknown to him, the angry crowd dragged his two friends outside the city gates.

"What is happening, God?" he begged. "Don't You seeing what's happening here? Paul can be abrasive, but he's Your servant. He's preaching about You. Aren't You going to protect him? Can't You send someone to rescue him?"

As he sat lost in grief and panic, someone approached him. Embarrassed and depressed, he didn't even look up, but just rested his head on his knees.

"You're a stranger here," a voice said.

Elihu said nothing.

"What brings you to our town? Do you have business here?"

Still he didn't answer.

"Come, come." The man shook him by the shoulders. "You can speak to me. No one will bother you. The crowd has left. They're outside the city walls right now, beating up those visitors. Are you with them?"

Glancing up at the man, Elihu nodded.

"Is your business here in this town just to cause a riot?"

Elihu shook his head. "No, they're Christians. They've come to tell people about Jesus of Nazareth, but some of the Jews from

Iconium who were angry with them there have followed them here. The people here are confused."

"Yes, I know. They thought they were Zeus and Hermes. Are you a preacher too?"

"Oh, no. They brought me here because I was not safe in Jerusalem. I have an aunt who lives here."

"Really? What's her name?"

"She's—she's married to a Greek man now. Her name was Eunice when she was at home with my mother."

"Ah," the man said, "she married a Greek. Must have really upset your family."

"I don't know. I guess when she married him it did. But now that my mother and I are Christians, we consider Jews and Greeks as equals."

"Really? And you believe this?"

"Oh, yes."

"Then I will take you to your aunt Eunice. Your grandmother Lois is living with us too."

"Really? Living with 'us'? Are you . . . ?"

"I'm the Greek man that married your aunt Eunice. Come join us. We have a son your age. His name is Timothy. You two may get along pretty well."

"What about . . ." Elihu glanced toward the gate.

"I can't do anything about that right now. But I can get you out of here before they return. Now we should be moving."

"Yes, sir." Elihu jumped to his feet and followed his newfound uncle home.

VESTA

esta wrinkled her nose as she swept the soiled straw out of the jail cell. It was her least favorite chore, and she did it only on days when there were no prisoners, since the men could be dangerous. Fortunately, they never had long-term prisoners. Most people were either punished, executed, or freed, and long-term imprisonment was really not what the Philippi jail existed for.

"Thank the gods for that," she muttered as she kept sweeping. Prisoners were such filthy beings—although she supposed they couldn't help it. After all, if you had your feet in stocks and your wrists chained to the wall, there wasn't a lot you could do in terms of personal care and hygiene.

She swept the filthy, soiled straw out the door and spread clean straw in the cell. It was a fairly large room with iron rings on the walls so that they could accommodate several prisoners if they needed to. Usually, though, they had only two or three at a time.

Philippi was a fairly good place to live. The region had a lot of gold and silver mines and that had brought a lot of industry. Also it was a good place for Roman soldiers to retire when they finally finished their 25-year commitment to the empire. Then they were able to take their money and start a family.

It was the leading Roman colony in the region and the gateway between Greece and Italy. The people of Philippi tried to outdo Rome in their dress and manners and culture and felt that they were just as important as the empire's capital, especially considering their political and military history.

In spite of being a fairly important city, few Jews had settled in Philippi. Vesta had never met any until this week. Then she had encountered several down by the river, mostly women. She had heard of Hebrews before, and she had met Romans who had served in Palestine. But she just had never met any real Jews.

Vesta stepped out of the jail cell into the warm sunshine and continued to sweep her smelly pile over to the corner of the courtyard by the wall. It was the place where they burned trash. Hanging the broom on its hook, she hurried back to the kitchen.

"I'm all done," she said. "May I go down by the river now?"

Her mother nodded absentmindedly.

"Great," the girl said. "I'll see you at suppertime."

She headed for the river. A wealthy woman from Thyatira would gather with her friends down there every seventh day. Today was the seventh, Saturn's day, and she was looking forward to seeing them again. Vesta had learned that any town that had more than 10 Jews—well, more than 10 Jewish men—would build a synagogue to meet in. But Philippi did not have even 10 male Jews, so the little group would meet by the river on Sabbaths. Vesta was glad they did. She wasn't sure her father would be pleased with her attending some kind of Jewish temple, or synagogue, as they called it. But nobody minded her sitting down by the river talking to other women.

As she approached the riverbank she heard the wealthy woman say, "Look, here's our little friend, the jailer's daughter. She came back to be with us."

"My name is Vesta," she said.

"We're glad you came back. My name is Lydia."

"You're the woman from Thyatira that sells purple."

"Yes, that's what I do."

"My father says it's unusual that you moved here from Thyatira."

Lydia laughed. "Well, it was for business reasons. Many sell dyes in Thyatira, but no one else sells purple in Philippi."

"I'll tell him that," the girl said. "That makes sense. And we're only 10 miles from the sea here, so you can still get your murex shells brought here and do your crushing and dying here in Philippi."

"Right, and because this is on the caravan lines between Greece and Italy, all kinds of fabrics come through here. We buy them from traders, dye them, and then resell them."

"For lots of money," Vesta added.

"Yes," Lydia smiled. "Because it takes so many murex shells to make just one little ounce of dye, purple cloth ranks right up there with gold. Even emperors and kings use it to pay tribute and taxes and temple gifts. It's as good as money in international trade."

Vesta sat down next to her. "I don't care much about international trade, but I love this purple fabric."

The woman laughed. "Everyone does. You will notice that Jews have at least one little thread of it running through their clothing somewhere."

"Really? Even poor ones?"

Lydia nodded. "Yes. The God of the Jews wanted all of us to know that we were a special royal people and so even the poorest people are supposed to have a least one thread running through their cloth, although many of them like to have a full deep bluish-purple stripe. But only royalty can afford to make whole garments out of it."

"I wish I was a Jew," the girl sighed.

"Your father would not be happy if he heard you say that."

"Why?"

"Oh, you know," Lydia replied. "Not everybody likes those who are different. I'm sure your father would be much more comfortable having you worshiping the local gods, but you're welcome to join us every Sabbath. We'd be glad to tell you more about what it's like being a Jew."

"I'll just pretend I'm one when I'm with you," Vesta said with a smile.

"Well, come meet my friends while you're pretending." She introduced the girl to several of the other women.

"Are they Jews too?" Vesta asked.

"Yes, although they have some new ideas that we've been talking about."

"What kind of new ideas?"

"Well, one of the things that distinguishes us as a people is that we are waiting for our Messiah to come, and when He does He will be our king. My new friends here have been telling me that the Messiah did come and that He was crucified in Jerusalem."

"Uh, probably the Roman leaders did it," Vesta said. "They're really not going to want a rival king."

"You're pretty smart for one so young. Anyway," Lydia continued, "my friends were going to tell me a little bit more about this person. I would like to hear the whole story, so that I can decide for myself whether I think He was really the Messiah or just another impostor. A number of people have already claimed to be the Messiah."

Vesta nodded. "Every country has someone showing up and pretending they're royalty. The only thing that men want more than money is power. It's ridiculous. I would rather just be wealthy and live here in Philippi. I wouldn't have to rule the world to be happy."

"Yes, men can be quite ambitious," one of Lydia's friends said. "But there are ambitious women out there too."

"I suppose so," Vesta sighed. "But not me. I would settle for just being rich."

They continued chatting for only a few minutes before a man approached with two strangers. The women stood to their feet.

"I was wondering when you were coming," Lydia commented to one of them.

"I'm sorry," he said. "I ran into these two men, we got to talking, and the time just slipped away from us. These men are from Jerusalem. Their names are Paul and Silas."

Paul shocked them by speaking directly to them. "Your husband tells me that you have already heard a little about Yeshua of Nazareth."

"Yes. We were just discussing Him. But we really need to know more."

"Well," Silas said, "perhaps the Lord sent us here to tell you. We are followers of His, and we can tell you whatever you want to know."

"You actually talk to women?"

The apostle smiled understandingly. "I know that a Pharisee normally wouldn't do that, but now that we are followers of Yeshua it doesn't matter whether people are Jews or Gentiles."

"Gentiles?" Vesta asked.

"Greeks are Gentiles," Lydia explained.

"Oh," the girl said, puzzled. "He said that almost as if it were a bad thing. I'm quite proud of being Greek."

Lydia smiled at her. "I'm sure you are. Most Greeks are. But we're all women, and usually in the Jewish synagogues the women sit in a different part than the men, and the men don't actually talk to us."

Vesta frowned. "I don't think I'd like a religion like that. At our temple the women are the most important. They're the priestesses—"

"Yes," Lydia interrupted, "so they are. But let's see what Paul has to say to us." She turned back to the other men.

I laughed. As a human Lydia was quite diplomatic, but many Jews didn't even associate with Greeks, much less one who wanted to speak about what went on in their places of worship. Yet she was kind to the girl.

The small group sat down on the banks together with Paul and Silas who took turns telling the story of Jesus. Suddenly a loud shriek interrupted them.

"Oh, Demos and his fortune-telling woman," Vesta squealed. "This is great. If you give him a coin, she will tell you a secret about yourself that no one knows. Does anybody have any money?" She glanced around at her newfound friends. No one was reaching for their coin pouch.

The fortune-telling woman approached them. Suddenly she pointed at Paul and Silas and announced, "These men are servants of the most high God."

"She's telling you a secret without even charging you," the girl said, delighted. "Which god is that? Who is the most high God?"

"It is Jehovah," Paul explained. "But I don't know why she is saying this. She's been following us for days."

The woman began to shout louder. "These men are servants of the most high God. They have come to tell you what is true."

Lydia raised an eyebrow. "Should we believe someone like her?"

Fortunetellers had not been allowed in Israel, and the laws of Moses had told them in no uncertain terms not to have anything to do with them.

"She has an evil spirit in her," Silas replied. "That's what's making her able to see the future and say these things. It is not of God, yet she's telling the truth. Perhaps in the presence of the Holy Spirit the demon has less power."

Paul stood up. "We should ask the spirit to free her." He strode over to her.

"Be careful; don't touch her," Vesta cautioned. "Nobody can ever touch her. She goes really crazy if someone does."

Paul smiled at the girl and laid his hands on the fortuneteller's head. "In the name of Yeshua of Nazareth I command you to come out of her," he said in a strong voice.

Suddenly the woman screamed and fell to the ground.

"She looks as though she has the falling sickness," Lydia said.

"I think it's the demon," another woman in the group suggested. "I think it will stop in a minute when it leaves her."

Paul and Silas continued to command the spirit in the name of Yeshua. Suddenly the woman lay still. The other women rushed to her. "Here, let us help you sit up. Do you need a sip of water?"

The woman had lost her wild-eyed look. She looked much younger, although dirty and tired. "What happened to me?"

"You've just been delivered from a demon," Lydia's husband explained. "These two men prayed to the God Jehovah to free you."

"Well," said one of the men who had been accompanying the fortuneteller, striding up on his long legs, "you haven't done her any favors."

"Really?" Paul replied, standing up to his full height, which was just up to the other man's chest.

"Look at her," the other man complained. "She doesn't have the spirit anymore."

"Exactly," Paul said. "She's been delivered."

The tall man snorted. "You don't understand. That's how she makes her living. And it's how *I* make *my* living. The demon has obviously left her. She has no second sight anymore. Now she's useless to us."

He aimed a swift kick at the woman, and she curled up in a ball on the ground.

Silas stood to his full height and faced the fortuneteller's master. "You have used her long enough and abused her," he said. "But you won't anymore. While you may have lost your source of income, she has gained her freedom."

"Nonsense!" the man yelled. "She has no way of supporting herself. Now she'll starve, and let's see if she'll be grateful to you."

They angrily hurried off.

Lydia put her arms around the woman. "Don't listen to him. Come home with us. We'll take care of you."

About that time two more men approached them along the riverbank.

"Oh, look," Paul said. "Here are the rest of our friends."

Vesta glanced up.

"This," Paul said, turning to the other man, "is Luke, a physician who travels with me now too."

"Which is a good thing," Silas laughed. "As often as Paul gets beaten up, he needs his own physician along with him."

"The Lord knew that would be important," Paul agreed, "and I'm really grateful for it."

After Paul started telling stories it seemed as if hardly any time had passed until they noticed a group of angry men hurrying toward them. Vestra drew back by instinct, putting space and people between her and the little knot of believers. The recently healed fortune-telling woman cowered on the ground in fear. Shouting and shoving, the men grabbed Paul and his friend Silas. Vesta leaped back and ran for home as fast as she could. Surely her father could do something to help her friends.

I smiled to myself. Vesta still believed her father could do anything. One of the most painful things young people go through is realizing that their parents are just people and not the all-powerful individuals they once thought them to be. Unfortunately, this often makes them cynical, and then it is hard for them to accept that their heavenly Father really is all-powerful and really can fix anything.

The guardians moved into the violent knot of men. They had instructions to prevent any permanent or serious injuries to Paul and Silas. Snarling, the enemy agents pulled back. While they claimed control of the angry men, they were afraid of the gleaming guardians.

Vestra burst into her family courtyard. "Father! Father! You've got to come quickly! My friends are in trouble, and I think they are getting beaten up by a crowd of rough men! Father! Please do something!"

Her father listened with concern, then said, "You stay here in the house with your mother, and I will see what's happening."

"No, I want to come," she protested. "I want to know what happens to them. They're my friends."

Her father looked at her sharply. "I will check on what's happening, and I will also find out whether it is appropriate for you to be friends with such people. You need to be more careful, Vesta. What have we told you about speaking to strangers?"

The girl hung her head. "But these are nice people. You would really like them. They tell the most wonderful stories."

"You stay here with your mother," he said as he rushed away.

Vesta sat down next to her mother, who was stirring a thick stew bubbling over the fire. She looked at the clear blue sky. It was a beautiful day, yet horrible things were happening. It didn't seem right.

"God of Lady Lydia and her friends," she whispered, "are You there?" She heard no answer. "We need Your help. Paul and Silas are Your friends. They need You right now. Please help them."

As she wondered if their God heard her she sat and squirmed. It seemed as if Father had been gone forever. What was happening? Had Paul's God listened? Would He do anything to help His follower?

"Does Father have any other prisoners today?" she asked her mother.

"Yes," her mother said. "While you were gone they brought two different men in. One of them was from a group of merchants who had come through. He's been accused of killing his partner and taking the money. The other one is a thief—Timus."

"Timus is in for stealing *again*? After how badly they beat him last time, you'd think he wouldn't do that anymore."

"If he had any sense, he wouldn't," her mother agreed. "Some people just keep stealing no matter what the consequences are."

Vesta sighed. "It doesn't make any sense. His family has enough money. He has enough food. It's not as if he's hungry and trying to feed his family."

Her mother nodded. "Perhaps it's just the excitement of trying to get away with it. But the consequences are worse each time."

Poor Timus, Vesta thought. *I wonder what's wrong with him to make him keep doing that. Surely no one with any sense would keep doing such a thing if they didn't have to.*

By now it seemed like hours since Father had left. Ari, her uncle who watched the jail and helped Father with his chores, came out and sat with them.

"How is everything in there?" Mother asked.

"The same as always," Ari said. "Everyone always spends a great amount of energy trying to convince me of their innocence, as if I have anything to do with whatever happens to them. I'm only here to keep them here until the magistrates decide." He laughed. "They think I have more power than I really do." He stood. "Sounds as if some commotion is coming down the road."

Vesta jumped to her feet. "Maybe it's Father."

"Well, if it is," her uncle replied, "he's bringing a lot of friends with him."

I smiled. The men coming with him would hardly qualify as friends, but he definitely wasn't alone.

The crowd approached the house. Paul and Silas now had their hands bound, and the same angry men who had accosted them at the river now shoved them along.

They dragged Paul and Silas over to the large post in the center of the courtyard and looped the rope around their wrists up through the ring at the top. Then they pulled it tight, stretching the men until Paul had to stand on his tiptoes.

"Oh, no," Vesta moaned. "They're going to beat them."

"Go in the house, Vesta," her father said.

"But they're my friends," she protested.

"All the more reason. Go in the house and stay there until I come for you."

"You can't beat them, Father—they're good men."

He frowned. "This is my job, Vesta. I don't want to hear any more from you." Then he emphatically pointed to the door.

She knew better than to say anything more. Quickly she went into the living quarters for the jailer's family. There she put her hands over her ears. Even being inside wouldn't keep her from hearing everything that went on.

The shouts of men outside could not drown out the sound of the rod whistling through the air and biting into the backs of the men stretched on the whipping post.

"God of Paul and Silas," she whispered, "do You see what's happening? Do something."

I hovered in frustration. The guardians were close by, but they had no authorization to intervene. I knew that the faith of the two missionaries was strong enough to withstand any beating that these Philippian magistrates could administer, but what about the tender budding faith of this young girl? If the guardians did not intervene, would she lose her newly blossoming faith in Yeshua and the Mighty One? I shook my head. Of course not. The Mighty One always knew exactly what was happening and what He was doing. I just needed to be patient and see how He was going to bring honor and glory out of this terrible situation.

The beating seemed to last forever. Finally the noise in the courtyard faded away and things were quiet. Vesta's father had not returned to tell her that she could come out, and she knew better than to slip out on her own. She paced the floor in frustration. What was happening to her new friends? The girl could not hear any moaning. Had they killed them?

Pausing, she thought about the two men. The taller one seemed pretty tough and healthy, but the short, older man already walked as if he always hurt. Silas mentioned that he had been beaten before, and she had noticed that all the joints on his hands seemed swollen and gnarled.

She frowned. *It's wrong to hurt somebody that is already uncomfortable,* she thought. *These men are so mean.*

Her father finally came in after what seemed like an eternity. Vesta jumped up from the stool she was sitting on. "Are they all right?"

Father nodded. "Yes, they're in the jail now with their feet in stocks. It'll take them a little while to get over this, so I'm giving them some time alone together. Then later I'll take them a little water."

Vesta and her mother had been in the jail before to help clean it, but only when no prisoners were there. Father or Uncle Ari were the only ones who went in when it was occupied.

"It's just not a safe place for women to go," her father had often said, and she believed him. Most of the people who got put in there were extremely angry, and even if they had been good people before, by the time they had been accused and beaten and locked in a cell, they were ready to lash out at anybody who came near them.

It was the custom to beat any non-Romans and lock them up overnight before they faced the magistrates for the actual trial. Beating them often helped get details that the authorities used for evidence in the trial.

Vesta knew she couldn't go into the jail, but she crept over and sat down against the stone wall right below the ventilation slits (they were too small to be called windows). She hoped she could hear something from inside that would let her know her friends' condition. Soon voices cane through the slits.

"Are you able to move, my friend?" It sounded like Silas.

"Oh, a little bit," Paul responded.

"Do you have any broken bones?"

"Not this time. At least I don't think so."

"Well, that's a relief. Because of the odd positions of your legs, I couldn't tell."

"These stocks are designed that way to make people uncomfortable in case the beating didn't do it."

Silas started to chuckle, then groaned. "Well, they could have saved their energy then, because I think that the beating accomplished its mission just fine."

Vesta couldn't believe that Silas was actually making a joke about it. How could they when they must be hurting terribly?

"I guess if I had told them that I was a Roman, they wouldn't have beaten me," Paul said, "but I was afraid they'd give you both of our beatings if I did that."

"You're a Roman citizen? I wish I had known. I'm a Roman too, but I didn't want *you* to be the only one getting a beating."

The two men somehow laughed.

How can they laugh? Vesta thought. *They went through all of that for nothing.*

"Well, next time," Paul said, "we'll speak up now that we both know. I guess we should have discussed such things earlier in the trip."

It was quiet for a few minutes, and then Silas started humming.

"Oh, I know that one," Paul said, and the two men began to sing.

"'Not for our sake, God, no, not for our sake, but for your name's sake, show your glory.'"

They're singing, Vesta thought to herself. *How can they sing after all of this?*

Admittedly their voices were a little shaky. "'Do it on account of your merciful love, do it on account of your faithful ways. Do it so none of the nations can say, "Where now, oh where is their God?"'"

That's exactly what she had been praying, Vesta realized. Somehow she felt embarrassed. These men could go through all of that and still sing to their God. She shouldn't be asking whether He could hear or not. Obviously He was giving them the courage to handle their predicament.

"'Our God is in heaven doing whatever he wants to do. Their gods are metal and wood, handmade in a basement shop: carved mounts that can't talk, painted eyes that can't see, tin ears that can't hear, molded noses that can't smell.'"

Vesta's eyes opened wide. It was true!

"'Hands that can't grasp,'" they continued, "'feet that can't walk or run, throats that never utter a sound. Those who make them have become just like them, have become just like the gods they trust'" (Psalm 115:1-8, Message).

Suddenly a feeling of peace flooded her. No matter what the people of her city did to the prisoners, their God was taking care of them. She wished that she could have a faith as strong as Paul and Silas had.

I must tell Lydia, she thought. Then she went to let her mother know where she was going.

The singing went on late into the night.

"I wish they would shut up," Uncle Ari growled. "All that Jewish music is driving me crazy."

Vesta grinned to herself. She liked their singing. As long as they continued, she knew that their God was still taking care of them. It might be the middle of the night, but anybody who had been beaten never slept much. She raised up on her elbow to listen better to the words.

"'Hallelujah! You who serve God, praise God! Just to speak his name is praise! Just to remember God is a blessing—now and tomorrow and always. From east to west, from dawn to dusk, keep lifting all your praises to God'" (Psalm 113:1-3, Message).

Vesta thought about the words. "Just to speak His name is praise," she whispered in the darkness. "God of Lydia, God of Paul and Silas."

"'God is higher than anything and anyone, outshining every-thing you can see in the skies. Who can compare with God, our God, so majestically enthroned, surveying His magnificent heavens and earth? He picks up the poor from out of the dirt, rescues the wretched who've been thrown out with the trash.'"

"And takes care of prisoners who get beaten," the girl told herself.

"'Seats them among the honored guests,'" the men went on, "'a place of honor among the brightest and best. He gives childless cou-ples a family, gives them joy as the parents of children. Hallelujah'" (verses 8, 9, Message).

What a wonderful God! If people just knew about Him, she thought, *they wouldn't be able to help but like Him. All they would have to do is just hear about Him and they would be drawn to Him because of His goodness and His kindness.* He seemed like a divine version of her father.

She turned over, trying to find a more comfortable position. As she was just drifting off to sleep she heard a rumble. It seemed far away at first, but it grew closer and closer. What could it be?

It was now so loud that the ground was shaking. Mother's clay dishes stacked on the shelf fell with a crash, splintering broken pot-tery across the stone floor.

"It's an earthquake," she heard her father shout. "Everybody get outside before the roof falls in."

Uncle Ari reached Vesta first and scooped her up in his strong arms. They rushed outside. Just as they made it outside, the roof caved in with a crash. Clouds of dust obscured everything.

"The prisoners," Father gasped.

As the sound faded away and the ground stopped shaking, Father called for torches.

"Ari, light a torch. We have to see if the prison is still intact."

Could the ceiling have collapsed on the prisoners? If so, they could all be dead now. As Uncle Ari brought over two torches and

Father grabbed one, they saw that the entire roof was still intact, but chunks of the wall had broken way out and the men who had been chained to the wall and with their feet in stocks were not in the spot where Father had left them.

"They've escaped," he said in a dull voice. He had been holding his sword in the other hand ever since he had rushed outside with it. Now he walked over to the wall. Placing the handle against the wall, he pressed the tip against his chest.

"No, Father, stop!" his daughter shouted. "Don't do that!"

She knew that any jailer who allowed any prisoners to escape faced the death penalty. Father wasn't going to wait for the torture he would have to endure before it happened. He was leaning forward, getting ready to fall on the sword. Braced against the wall, it would go right through him.

"Father, stop, please don't," she sobbed.

Suddenly someone shouted from inside the prison. "Wait, don't hurt yourself. We're all here. The four of us. We haven't gone anywhere. Don't harm yourself. Bring your torch in here and count us. You'll see."

Her father slowly dropped his sword to his side.

"Come on," Ari said. "Let's go look."

The two men walked through the gap in the wall and glanced around the cell. Paul and Silas were standing right by the entrance in their bloodstained clothing. The accused murderer and thief were standing behind them, looking around in dazed shock and surprise.

"We are here," Paul repeated. "No one has escaped. Your life is not in danger. Don't harm yourself—your family needs you."

"I—I—uh—I don't know what to say," the father stammered.

"You can give thanks to God," Paul said. "The most high God."

"I—I will do that," the jailer replied. "Please come into the house. Oh . . ." he stopped.

They couldn't enter the front of the house. The roof had fallen in. They walked around to the side, only to have an aftershock make Father hesitate. "Perhaps we should remain in the open court-yard. Please sit," he said, motioning to some stone benches.

Paul and Silas sat down as if they were friends coming over for a dinner invitation. The other two prisoners, still shocked into si-lence, sat down too, though they kept glancing toward the court-yard gate.

Mother brought water. As Uncle Ari lit some oil lamps they re-alized that the men looked terrible. They were bruised with dried blood everywhere.

"Here," Mother said, "let's get these bloodstained clothes off."

They pulled their robes down around their waists, and she and Father and Uncle Ari took wet cloths and sponged off the dried blood and carefully bathed their wounds.

"I'm so sorry," Father murmured again and again. "I'm so sorry."

"You don't need to apologize anymore," Silas told him. "You were just doing your job. We hold nothing against you."

"Vesta was right," her mother observed. "She said you men were very different."

"What makes you unlike other prisoners?" Father asked. "Why are you like this? Why aren't you angry at us? And why didn't you escape?"

"Oh," Silas answered, "we were hoping you would ask."

"And so," Paul continued some time later, "after He had been dragged from place to place, roughed up and beaten by the soldiers, worn the crown of thorns and been forced to play the blindfolded prophet game, scourged, and now nailed to a cross, He still prayed, 'Father, forgive them; for they know not what they do.' If He could forgive them at that point, how could Silas and I hold a little beat-ing against you?"

"That's right," Silas added. "What's a little beating among friends!"

Father shook his head. "This Person sounds like a wonderful

being and totally unlike any of the other gods. What happened next?"

As Paul continued to tell about Yeshua the sky went from black to a rosy pink and then daylight as the jailer's family listened in fascination.

Suddenly Vesta's father stood. "I wish to be a follower of your God. What must I do?"

Paul and Silas broke into a huge smile. "Repent and be baptized," the smaller man explained. "Put away any wrongdoing, follow His rules for life, and worship Him."

"Can we be baptized at the river?" Father asked, putting his arm around Mother.

Vesta jumped up and stood on the other side of her father, slipping her arm around his waist. "Me too," she said.

"Of course," Father agreed.

"I also wish to follow your God," Uncle Ari added.

The two other prisoners who had said nothing the entire time painfully struggled to their feet. "Will you also baptize criminals?" the young thief asked.

Silas smiled. "Certainly. Not only will we baptize you as a follower of Jesus, but we will pray for the Holy Spirit to fill you and heal whatever you have inside of you that is causing you to steal continually. You will be healed, and you will no longer be a criminal. Becoming a follower of Christ gives you a brand-new start in life."

"Yes," Paul said. "Anyone who is in Christ becomes a totally new creature."

The young man broke into a smile.

The older prisoner stood stiffly. "I too wish to be baptized, though I refuse to repent of the crime I have been accused of. I didn't do it."

Paul nodded. "I know. And the Lord knows. He knows every secret of your heart. And He also knows how to influence the magistrates so that they will find the truth and set you free."

A look of great relief flooded over the older man's face.

"Well, what are we waiting for?" Father said. "Let's go down to the river."

"May I do something quickly?" Vesta inquired.

"What is it?" her father said.

"Could I run and get Paul and Silas's friends? I know where they live. I am sure they would love to be there for the baptism."

"Sure," Father told her. "You are so speedy on those little legs of yours, you'll probably be able to find the friends and still make it to the river before we do." He chuckled. "We should have named you 'Little Gazelle' instead of Vesta." Then he stopped. "Perhaps we should change your name."

Vesta laughed. "That would be fine. In the meantime I will go get the others."

Dion

(Corinth)

ion's breath came in ragged gasps as he continued to run as hard as he could in spite of the stabbing pain in his side. He was almost home. Janus, his cruel owner, was gaining on him. But he was almost there. If he could just get home, everything would be all right.

They had now entered the slums on the edge of town. He turned the last corner and stopped. Then he felt as if the bottom had dropped out of his world. The little shack that had been his family's home for almost a year stood empty with the door swinging open. How could they have left without him?

They had moved many times in his young life to escape creditors. Each time Father would say that they were going to get a new start in a new city and that he was not ever going to drink anymore and their new life would be a happy one.

It had always ended like this, but they had never left without him. Of course, Father had never sold him before, either.

The boy turned to look back just as Janus caught up with him. Dion felt a sickening thud as the man's fist connected with his face, and then everything went black.

My heart was breaking. Some of my assignments were extremely painful. As hard as it was for me to see the suffering of this young human, I knew that it was nothing compared to the heartbreak the Mighty One was experiencing. How He loved these frail creatures.

"Oh, that's real good, Janus. Knock him out cold. He'll really do a lot of work for you lying unconscious there."

The slave owner turned with a laugh. "Aquila, what are you doing in this poverty-stricken part of town?"

"Came to hire a couple of day workers. Priscilla and I have a large tent order."

Janus nodded. "I see. Well, I have a little runaway."

Dion could hear the conversation going on above him. Gradually things came back into focus.

"I think he's waking up," Aquila told Janus.

"He'd better," the boy's owner sneered.

"Come on, boy," he said, kicking him, "it's time to get up. You've got more work to do today."

Closing his eyes, Dion prayed to all the gods of Corinth at once. *Just let me die,* he prayed. *I just want to die.* He had never experienced so much pain and humiliation as he had during the past two weeks that he had belonged to Janus. He didn't even know people did such horrible things.

Apparently the gods of Corinth had other things on their mind. And whereas Dion had been afraid he was going to die at first, now he was afraid he wasn't going to—and the prospect of living was almost more than he could bear.

Aquila looked down at the boy. He might have been good-looking at one point, but now he was dirty, covered from head to toe with bruises of various colors. "What will you take for him?" he suddenly asked.

Janus turned to him with a sly smile. "Why, Aquila, I didn't know you were into . . ."

"I'm not," the tentmaker snapped. "But it looks as if your clients have beaten the life out of this lad, and if somebody doesn't buy him and feed him, he will die in your . . . care."

Janus shrugged. "This business has a high turnover. A lot of these kids don't live long. It's just an occupational hazard."

"So what will you take for him?" Aquila repeated.

Dion heard Janus quote a price three times what he had given his father the night they had made their deal.

For a moment Aquila hesitated, then gave him the money.

"Glad to do business with you," Janus said as he cheerfully walked down the street.

"Open your eyes. It's safe to get up now," Aquila said.

Janus turned and shouted, "Oh, by the way, he's mute and probably not too smart, but that's an advantage in our business." With a parting laugh he went on his way.

Aquila helped the boy to his feet, who took two or three steps, then crumpled back to the pavement. "Well, I can see you're not going to be able to make the walk home," he said.

Fortunately he was a large man. He scooped Dion up in his arms and with long angry strides headed toward home.

Dion kept his eyes closed. He didn't understand exactly what had just happened, but it couldn't be any worse than anything that had happened to him so far.

"Priscilla, I'm back. Come see what I've got."

As the beautiful woman entered the room Dion peeked through slitted eyes so she would think that they were still closed.

"Oh," she said. "I send you out for day laborers and to buy some more wool and this is what you come back with."

Dion's heart sank. Aquila put him down where he could lean against a wall.

"Janus was beating him in the street," he said.

"Poor little fella!" Priscilla exclaimed.

"So I bought him."

Priscilla nodded. "Good! Then he'll never have to go back to that again."

Never, the boy thought. It sounded good to him.

"How much did he charge you?"

Oh, no, Dion told himself. *She's going to be really upset.*

Aquila named the price, and Priscilla shook her head. "You have a tender heart, and that's why I love you so much. But what are we going to do now about this tent order? I suppose that we can do the work ourselves and not get day workers. It will just take us longer. But what are we going to do for the extra wool we need?"

Aquila shook his head. "I don't know. I just couldn't—I just couldn't leave him with Janus."

"Of course you couldn't. We'll have to ask the Lord to help us on this one, but I'm sure He wouldn't have wanted you to leave the child there."

"Here, let me look at you," she said to Dion. Lifting his chin, she looked into his eyes. They were red and puffy. She wiped a cool wet cloth over his face, being especially gentle with the bruises.

After she stood clicking her tongue and staring at him, she turned to Aquila. "This boy is half starved. We're going to need to feed him and take care of him for a while before he's going to be able to do much to help around here. I just can't imagine what horrible abuse he's been through."

Dion lowered his eyes. He didn't want her to be able to imagine what he had endured. In fact, he didn't want anyone to know.

"Don't you worry," she said. "We're going to get you cleaned up and feed you. It doesn't look as if anyone's done that in a while. Everything will be all right—you'll see."

Dion's eyes filled with tears. She sounded so much like his mother before she had become so discouraged with his father's drinking.

The boy was in the process of gobbling his third plate of food from Priscilla when they heard a knock on the door to the courtyard.

"We have visitors," Aquila announced, opening the door.

The boy saw several people—a woman and some men. Although he wanted to hide somewhere, he wasn't sure he could stand up. They came in and sat in the shade by him.

A pleasant courtyard, it consisted of two parts—the shaded area with the little ornamental fountain where the visitors sat, and the work area.

He guessed Priscilla and Aquila must be tentmakers, for they had heavy pieces of cloth spread out everywhere, and the material looked as if it were in the early stages of being stitched together.

"It's so good to see you," Priscilla exclaimed as she rushed over and hugged the woman who had accompanied the men. Then she turned to Dion. "This is my friend, Agia. Her husband, Crispus, is the head of the synagogue here in Corinth. Aquila and I are Jews. You've probably figured that out by now. Agia, this is Dion. Aquila brought him home this morning."

"What happened to him?" the woman asked.

"He's had some hard times lately," Priscilla replied evasively. "He was being beaten when my husband found him. Aquila bought him, so he's ours now."

The other woman smiled. "Well, I imagine his life will be much better here at your house."

Dion squirmed uncomfortably.

Priscilla noticed his reaction. "I'm sorry, Dion. We'll continue our discussion indoors and let you finish your dinner. Here, I have some honey cakes," she said, putting a plate down next to him.

The boy nodded, and the two women went inside the house.

Aquila and Crispus sat talking by the partially finished tent spread out in the work area. The other man with them was shorter and bald, and he walked as if his hip hurt. After a bit he wandered over next to Dion in the shade and sat down.

"I hear Priscilla and Aquila have taken you in," he said.

Taking another bite of stew, Dion said nothing.

"They took me in too," Paul continued.

The boy glanced at him in surprise.

"That's quite a bruise you have there. Does the rest of your body match it?"

Dion grimaced. His face was probably the least bruised part of his body.

"I understand completely. I've looked like that several times." He grinned at the boy. "Looking like that didn't bother me at all. It was feeling like that that I object to."

A smile played on the corner of Dion's lips. It was the first time he had smiled in weeks.

"Don't smile too much. You'll crack that scab in the corner of your mouth, and then it will bleed, and Priscilla will accuse me of hurting you. And then I'll be in real trouble."

Dion felt a little chuckle jiggling the inside of him. Whoever this guest of Priscilla and Aquila's was, he felt that they could be friends.

"I suppose I should introduce myself," the man said. "My name is Paul. I became a follower of Jesus of Nazareth, and I have been traveling round telling other people about Him. I started out mostly telling Jews about Him, but I guess Moses knew what he was talking about when he kept calling them a stiff-necked people. And they've given me a stiff neck several times."

The boy smiled. Most of the Jews he had met seemed pretty stubborn too.

"Now," Paul said, "everywhere I go I start out in the synagogues and tell the Jews about Him first. Some of them become followers, such as Crispus and his wife here. And some don't. And then if they don't beat me up and throw me out of town, I also go to the Gentiles and tell them."

Shyly Dion handed one of the honey cakes to Paul.

"Thank you," Paul said. "I'm starving. This looks good."

A warm glow spread through the boy. It had been a long time since he'd had a friend.

"Aquila says the man who sold you to him told him that you're a mute. Is that true?"

Dion stared at the ground and didn't answer. He hadn't spoken since the day his father had sold him. Did that make him a mute? He wasn't sure.

"Did they cut your tongue out?"

The boy shook his head. Then he stuck his tongue out to show Paul that it was intact.

The apostle smiled. "Well, you seem to understand perfectly, so you're definitely not deaf. And I think that if your tongue is still in there, perhaps you will talk when you are ready."

By now Crispus and Agia were saying goodbye to Priscilla and Aquila.

"Thank you so much," said Aquila, "and we'll see you in a couple days."

The other couple waved goodbye, then left.

Priscilla and Aquila joined Paul and Dion in the shade.

"Now that our friends are gone," Paul said, "why don't you two tell me what the problem is? I can see it written all over your faces."

"Really?" Priscilla asked.

"Yes, so tell me. Perhaps I can be of assistance."

"I'm not sure how you can help us. And you're a guest in our home. We shouldn't trouble you with our personal matters."

"Nonsense. Tell me what's bothering you."

"It's my fault," Aquila explained. "I went into Corinth today, to the market, to hire a day worker to help us because we have a large tent order. I also needed to buy some more wool for tent fabric because we did not have enough to cover the order we have."

"Go on," Paul urged.

"This slave master who is known all over Corinth for the poor treatment he gives to his slaves was chasing this young one, and had just caught him. I couldn't just stand there and watch him beat a child who has already apparently been abused many times before. So I bought Dion and brought him home."

The boy shifted uncomfortably again. He felt badly that his purchase had caused a hardship to the people who had been so kind to him.

"Is that the whole problem?" Paul persisted. "Is that all there is?"

The couple nodded.

"Well, I am a tentmaker. I have been all my life. My father made sure that I had some practical training in case something ever happened. The beating I took in Phillipi has left my hands pretty crippled, but I can do the large work as long as you don't ask me to do the stitching part."

"Oh, we couldn't let you do that," Priscilla protested. "You're our guest."

"Oh, nonsense. Those who don't work shouldn't eat."

Dion squirmed awkwardly.

Paul turned to him. "Don't get scared, little friend. When I was recovering from my thumpings, nobody made me work until I was able to move again. No one is threatening to starve you here."

"Absolutely not," Aquila agreed. "You can work when you feel better. But for now you just need to rest and eat and heal."

Priscilla's eyes filled with tears. "Oh, Paul, you are such a good friend. What would we do without you?"

"Well, I'm not finished yet. The money for the wool . . ."

The couple looked up at him.

"Before I left Philippi, Lydia, a wealthy supporter of the believers, gave me some money to help us get started here in Corinth."

"But we couldn't take your money," she protested.

"Absolutely not," Aquila added.

"Well, can either of you write?"

Aquila looked at the ground. "I never excelled in studies, but"—and he looked proudly at his wife—"Priscilla can write. Not many women have had a chance to learn, but she reads and writes very well."

"Well, I wish to send some letters to some of the other groups of believers, and if Priscilla will take dictation and write the letters for me, I will give you the money you need for the wool."

As the days passed, the tentmaking process fascinated Dion. They took the wool that Aquila had bought in the market, spread it out, sprayed it with some mixture that Priscilla made, and let it dry in the sun. Then they rolled it and flattened it and dried it again until instead of a smelly and fluffy pile, it was a thin, heavily matted felt that could keep sun and rain out.

The three adults worked together, pulling the big pieces into position, attaching them in the right spots, and stitching the rope loops where they belonged.

Dion steadily grew stronger. His bruises faded, and he wasn't as dizzy when he stood up. Sometimes he helped pull the large pieces of heavy felt and held them in place.

During the heat of the day they would all sit in the shady area, and Paul would dictate letters to other groups of believers. The boy listened in fascination. The things Paul said were unlike anything he had ever heard. But then these people were different from any he had ever met, so that shouldn't have been a surprise.

Sometimes at nighttime when Priscilla and Aquila had retired to their chambers he and Paul would lie on the rooftop enjoying the cool breeze, and the man would tell him stories about Jesus. Dion thought he would have really liked this Jesus person. He must have been as nice as Paul. It puzzled him how anyone could have not liked Him, for if they had just gotten to know Him and seen what He was like, they would have loved Him. It horrified Dion when

Paul told him how Jesus' enemies had Him put to death; then the boy felt great delight when the little man told him that God had raised Him back to life.

It disappointed him that he lived in Corinth, so far from Jerusalem and Nazareth, but then he had been born too late anyway. Jesus had gone back to His Father a long time before Dion had ever been thought of. He wondered how Jesus would feel about him.

Paul must have sensed the boy's question, for he raised up on his elbow and looked him right in the eye. "Dion, don't be afraid. The Lord loves you. He knows you inside and out."

The boy shuddered.

"He knows everything about you, but He's willing to heal it and take away the painful things and fill you with His joy. Anybody who's in Christ is a new creature. All those things are gone and it's as if they never happened."

Dion's heart swelled with hope and his eyes widened.

"It's true," Paul insisted. "I suppose you're wondering how someone becomes a follower of Jesus. You just need to repent and be baptized as you turn away from your former life and begin to live for Christ."

The boy looked questioningly at him.

"Ah, you want to know about being baptized. Perhaps there will be other believers and you can see a baptism. We lead them into the water and then gently lower them as if they're being buried. It's as if their whole old life has died and gone away. Everything that has happened to them before—all the pain, all the shame, anything they've ever gone through. The old life is buried. Then we raise them up out of the water, and they are brand-new, fresh and clean. They have a new start. Nothing that ever happened before matters. Now they are followers of Christ."

Dion sat up. It sounded wonderful. He put his hands to his chest.

"Yes, you," Paul said. "Even you. We are all sinners, you know.

I was one of the worst sinners, and I'm ashamed of my life before I met Jesus. I wasn't just a sinner myself—I helped hurt and even kill many of Jesus' followers. And yes, He forgave even me and gave me a new life. How could I not love Him?"

When Dion tried to speak, it had been so long since he had done so that all that came out was a funny noise. He put his hand on his chest again.

"Are you saying you want to be a follower of Christ?"

The boy nodded vigorously.

"Do you wish to be baptized?"

Again Dion bobbed his head.

"Well, that certainly can be arranged. We will take care of it first thing tomorrow."

He slid over and hugged Dion. The boy's first impulse was to pull back and freeze, then suddenly he remembered that he was among friends. No one was going to hurt him here. And receiving a hug from Paul was a friendly, loving thing, not something that was a prelude to pain. He held his arms out, stiffly at first, and hugged Paul back.

Over breakfast the following morning Paul told Priscilla and Aquila of Dion's decision. The boy nodded his head in agreement as the apostle told them of his desire to be baptized as a follower of Christ.

"Oh, that is wonderful," Priscilla exclaimed. She hugged Dion, then said, "I must go over to Agia's house and let them know. They can notify the rest of the believers so that we can meet down by the river on Sabbath instead of at the synagogue. They have been speaking with a man named Stephanus and his family about Jesus too. Perhaps they will want to be baptized at the same time. This is wonderful, Dion. Now you will always have a family, because the believers are family and you will have some wherever you go."

"It has certainly been that way for me," Paul agreed. "I have family in many towns."

A smile blazed across Dion's face. He had felt abandoned before. Now he never had to be alone again.

Paul looked over at him. "I will set aside some time every day, during the evening before we go to sleep, to tell you stories of Jesus and His followers. The more you hear, the more you will love our God, who sent His Son to us. And the more you learn about Him, the more you can share with others."

Dion raised his eyebrows. How could he share with others?

"Don't worry," Paul added. "When the time is right, the Lord will let you know how to do it. He has a place for everyone in His family. We call ourselves the body of Christ. Every body part is important. The various parts are used for different purposes. If you just wait, the Lord will show you what role He wants you to play in the body. You are as important as any other member."

Aquila nodded. "That's right. Becoming part of the body of Christ, you're now adopted into His family. Christ called us all His brothers and sisters. That means you are a brother of Christ and therefore a son of the King, the Almighty, the King of kings of the entire universe. You're royalty now."

As they sat in the shade that afternoon, Paul and Priscilla talked while Aquila leaned against a bale of wool, snoring quietly.

"You have been wonderful to write down all these things for me, Priscilla," Paul said. "I appreciate it greatly. Now we can send that letter off to the believers in Rome. I hope to visit them someday soon, but for now at least I can send them letters."

"When are you going to go see them?" she asked.

"Well, I'm hoping to go to Spain after I deliver the rest of this money to Jerusalem that I have from Lydia and the believers there. I thought I could go to Rome on the way to Spain."

"I hope you stay here a while before you go there," she said. "Our little group of believers is just getting started. We need you here."

"I plan to stay here at least a year to help this congregation get on its feet. I won't move on till then."

Priscilla smiled. "Good. You know you are welcome here in our home as long as you choose to stay in Corinth. Do you have another writing project in mind?"

"Actually, I do. I'm just not sure how to go about it."

"What do you mean?"

"I want to write a letter to the Jewish believers to explain our belief in Christ. To show how He is our high priest and how He fulfills all of the Jewish stories and tradition."

"That's a wonderful idea."

"Well, yes and no," he said. "It's something that I feel I need to do, yet . . ."

"Yet what? You're educated as a Pharisee. Surely you're the perfect person to write such a thing, especially to those who have not yet accepted Yeshua. You can do it in a way that they will understand."

"But so many hate me," he sighed. "And because I was so well known as a Pharisee, they will recognize my style. They hate me in Jerusalem. They're not going to accept anything if they know it's from me."

Priscilla thought a moment. "I guess I can understand their reaction.

"What if you wrote it?"

She laughed. "What synagogue is going to be willing to be taught by a woman?"

They both sat in silence.

"We could send it anonymously," Paul suggested, "but they would still recognize my style. Wait, I've got an idea. We can discuss these things, but if you write them in your own words, Priscilla, it will be in your style. Then we will send it and won't say who wrote it. I will tell you the things on my heart, and it will be our combined project."

Priscilla clapped her hands. "Do you think it will work? Do

you think they will accept it?"

"I don't know, but I don't think the Holy Spirit would be urging us to do something that there wasn't a great need for."

I nodded as I watch them. The Almighty never leads His children to do anything without a reason. No act prompted by Him is ever wasted energy, and certainly this writing project would not be.

Dion loved to listen to Paul and Priscilla as they prepared letters for the other believers. He felt as if many of the things they said were about him and fit his own life. The letter they had been working on and finished the night before had had things in it that he felt were about him, and he tried to remember every word. Words such as "everything that happens, works together for good to those who love God." Even the horrible things in his life had led to his living with Priscilla and Aquila. Perhaps it had all worked together for good. Perhaps this God had seen him even back before he had even known there was one true God, and had guided him along the way and kept him alive so that he could learn about Him.

Priscilla and Paul talked on about the things they would put into the book. All these people they were discussing who had acted on faith—who were they? Intently listening, he cocked his head to one side. Paul glanced at him.

"Ah," he said, "our young friend wants to know who all these people are."

Dion nodded.

"Priscilla will continue to write them down. Then I will bring the scroll up with us this evening and I will tell you about each one of them. There's a fascinating story behind each person. None of them were perfect, and yet each one of them acted on faith, and God considered them as belonging to His people."

"Even some of them who made big mistakes," Priscilla added. "It's very encouraging to know that God's people were all human beings just like us."

The boy smiled. He hoped Paul never ran out of stories.

Every day now he eagerly helped with the tentmaking so that they would have more time later for stories. Paul told them about Abel and how his brother Cain killed him for doing exactly what God said. He heard the story of Enoch, a man who walked so closely with God that he skipped death entirely.

One of his favorites was the story of Noah, a man who lived in the middle of dry land and yet whom God instructed to build a huge boat. His family were the only ones who believed him and who boarded the boat when He said to. And animals of every kind came and boarded it with them, as though the Lord had rounded them up Himself. Then came a great flood that destroyed all the people who had not listened, even though God had patiently told them for 120 years that it was going to happen.

Then Paul told of Abraham. God called him away from a comfortable life to be a nomad in the desert. And of his wife Sarah, who finally had a son when she was an old woman because God could give a child to anyone He wished.

Feeling Priscilla's gaze on him, Dion looked up at her. Her eyes were filled with tears. She and Aquila turned, and their eyes met.

"Dion," Aquila said, "we want you to think about something."

What is it? he wondered.

"Priscilla and I would like to adopt you as our own son. We've been married many years, but as you can see, we have no children. You fit in well with us, and you seem to enjoy working with us on the tents, so we would like to adopt you legally. Then you could be a permanent part of the family and inherit our tentmaking business when we become too old to do it. Would you be willing to be adopted as our son?"

The boy's mouth dropped open in shock. Did these people really want to adopt him? They knew where he came from—the kind of life they had purchased him out of.

"Do you understand the adoption process?" Aquila asked. "We would go to the Roman magistrate and fill out the appropriate papers. That would make you legally our son. It means that all these stories we have told you would be about people in your family tree, for once you are adopted it's as if we had given birth to you and you had always been here. You'll be a legal part of our family."

Dion started to cry. He didn't want to—it just welled up from deep inside him. His reaction startled Aquila, but Priscilla rushed over and wrapped her arms around him and rocked him back and forth. As he clung to her all the hurts and all the pain of losing his family, all the horror and loneliness that he had experienced as a slave, all gurgled out in tears and shuddering sobs.

The boy cried until it seemed there was nothing left inside of him. Priscilla still held him close, still rocking him gently. She stroked his hair back out of his face.

"There, there," she said, "a good cry can be really healing."

When he finally slipped into an exhausted silence, she tipped his face up toward hers and looked into his eyes.

"You are my son," she said. "Nothing will ever make me love you any less. And nothing that ever has happened or ever will happen to you will make me stop loving you. Aquila and I will love you as long as we live for you are our son."

Dion gave a trembling smile.

"It's getting late in the day," Aquila said. "We will go to the magistrate tomorrow morning. And we'll take Paul with us as a witness for the legal papers."

"Now," Priscilla added, "how about some supper before we all starve to death?"

Dion was awake early Sabbath morning. Today he would be baptized and become a legal adoptee in the family of God, just as he had been legally adopted by Priscilla and Aquila the day before.

The small group of believers met on the edge of the river. Paul spoke to them for a few minutes and then introduced Dion and Stephanus. Then he led them into the water. Paul baptized Stephanus first and then the boy.

Today I'm going to be new, he thought. *I will let go of all those horrible things and never think of them again, for in Christ I'm going to be a new creature.*

As the cold water closed over his face he felt excitement tingling through his whole body. And as he came up out of the water he felt the joy bubbling up.

"Oh, thank You, God," he said in a rusty voice.

Everyone started and stared at him.

"I thought he was mute," one member whispered to another.

Dion paid no attention at all. "Oh, thank You, God," he said. "Thank You so much. Thank You for giving me a family and letting me be part of Your family. Thank You for making me a whole new life."

Paul stood in the water, smiling. "I knew the Lord would give you a voice when He was ready for you to speak," he told the boy. "Now let's get out of this chilly river and put on some dry clothes before we chat with His family." Then they climbed up the bank.

LUCAS

(Ephesus)

ucas stretched and wiped the perspiration off his face with the kerchief he carried in his loincloth. He didn't wear much more than that while he was working. It was too hot next to the big fires. He took a long drink of water from the communal dipper in the drinking bucket and returned to his task at hand. Even though he was only 14, he was already becoming a skilled metalworker. He had been apprenticed to Demetrius the silversmith for two years now and learned quickly.

"We're ready to pour," Demetrius shouted. "Are the molds ready?"

"Yes, sir," he replied. He had cleaned each mold and polished the inside so that there was no fleck of dust or other debris sticking to the surface that would cause a mar or bump in the silver statue of Diana. "It took me a little longer today on a couple of these, but I think it will be worth it."

The silversmith nodded. "Your careful work with the molds saves us a lot of time during the casting."

The lad smiled to himself. He worked hard and was careful with details, and it felt good to him that his boss noticed and appreciated that.

Now he helped Demetrius pour the molten silver into the molds. Today they were making the smallest-size figures, so they had many more molds to fill. It took a lot more effort than casting a larger statue. And it was important not to spill any of the precious metal on the ground. Even more vital was not spilling any on the workers. Hot metal could cause serious burns that could disfigure people forever.

"That's it," Demetrius said after a while. "Let's call it a day. You've worked hard. Go have some fun."

"Yes, sir," the boy replied. He didn't have to be told twice. That was another thing he liked about working for Demetrius. He worked hard, but the man was fair and gave everyone time off in the heat of the day if their tasks were done.

The other workers had been polishing the statues that had been cast the day before. As soon as they finished, Demetrius allowed them to leave also.

Lucas wandered down the main thoroughfare in Ephesus. Life was good. He came from a good family and worked for a good boss. When his apprenticeship ended he would be a silversmith in his own right.

Ephesus was a great place to live. With about 300,000 people in it, it was one of the largest cities in the Roman Empire. It had count-less monuments, theaters, and temples. And, of course, it was the headquarters for the worship of Diana (or Artemis, as some people called her, depending on whether they were Greek or Roman). He knew that in years past she had gone by other names, too. And the worship of another goddess had been incorporated into her cult, but that was just good business. Ephesus was where the sacred stone statue of Diana had floated down from heaven and she had been worshiped there ever since—or so the story went. Lucas didn't care as long as lots of people bought statues of her.

He stopped in the Agora to watch a show with two trained apes from Africa. He couldn't help laughing out loud at their antics. Glancing over, he noticed another boy his own age also laughing at the apes. They made eye contact.

"Hello," Lucas said.

The other boy nodded.

"Aren't they great?"

The other boy nodded again. He seemed very shy. Then it looked as if he gathered all his courage and said, "Hi; my name is Dion."

"I'm Lucas."

The two boys began chatting and wandered through the Agora looking at the sights. The place had new and different things to see every day.

The tourist business was the biggest source of income in Ephesus. It brought many spectacles and other interesting things to watch.

"Are you hungry?" Lucas asked.

Dion nodded.

"Let's get something to eat." Lucas turned onto the street where his parents' home was. His mother greeted them at the gate to the courtyard.

"Mother, this is my friend Dion. I met him in the Agora."

"Welcome to our home, Dion."

"We came home 'cause we're kind of hungry," her son said.

"So what's new," she laughed. "You were born hungry and never got over it."

"And I don't plan to right now," Lucas added.

"Well, that's good," she replied, "because I just fixed all this stuff, and my feelings would be hurt if you didn't eat it."

Dion noticed that Lucas and his mother seemed really to enjoy each other's company. It made him long for his own mother. He wondered where she was now and if she missed him as much as he did her.

Lucas watched him as they ate. The boy wasn't just shy. He

seemed to have an inner sadness that kept creeping into his eyes. With a shrug Lucas decided that he would see if he could find out later what was bothering his new friend.

"What do you do?" he asked Dion.

"My parents are tentmakers," he said, "so I work with them on the tents. We do most of our work early in the day, when it's a little cooler. And then in the heat of the day they rest. I'm not much into naps, so they let me go out and wander."

"Yes, that's how my day goes," Lucas replied. "We start before light so that we can stoke up the fires and start melting the silver, and by the heat of the day we try to be finished. Then our master lets us go. We're really lucky. A lot of people our age work from sunup until it gets dark."

"I know. Many people have much harder lives than we do." He was going to say something else, but then stopped. "Thank you so much for the good food," he said to Lucas's mother when she came back.

She smiled. "I'm glad you enjoyed it. Now you two run along and do whatever you boys do in your spare time. I have things of my own to do."

"Where do you live?" Lucas asked a few minutes later. "Have you been here in Ephesus long? You're obviously not from here."

"How can you tell that?" he laughed. "We just came a few weeks ago, and we're renting a place not far from here. I'll show you."

The two boys walked toward the home of Aquila and Priscilla.

"Oh, look," Priscilla said as they entered the courtyard. "Dion is back."

"Yes, and here's my friend Lucas. I met him in the Agora. He's a silversmith's apprentice."

Priscilla smiled warmly at him. "You're welcome in our home. I'm glad you're meeting some friends your age," she added, smiling at Dion. "Come join us. We were just sitting down in the shade here and having something to eat with our friend Apollos. He's a preacher who has come to our synagogue, so we invited him home. I think you'll like him." She glanced at Dion. "He's another story-teller like Paul."

Dion broke into a wide grin. He could never hear too many of the little evangelist's stories.

"What kind of stories?" Lucas asked.

"A lot of Jewish ones," Dion replied. "Stories of things that happened to their ancestors. And a lot about their God and how He took care of the family over the years.

"Then," he added, "there are those stories about Jesus of Nazareth. Those are things that happened before I was born, but not that long ago. He was the Son of the one God, and He came to earth to tell people about how the God Jehovah really felt about them."

"Jehovah?" Lucas said. "Never heard of Him. Everyone here in Ephesus worships Diana."

"I've noticed that most people do," Dion replied, "but a few of us don't." He smiled.

"So tell me more about this Paul."

"What if we sit over here and see what this Apollos person has to say? Then I'll tell you all the stories you want to hear afterward."

They joined Priscilla and Aquila and her friend Apollos in the shady part of the courtyard.

The man was already midstory. "And so John came to the Jordan River. A powerful preacher, he was not shy at all about pointing out the sins of the people listening to him. He charged the Romans to be fair and to be content with the wages they received. And he accused the religious leaders of being snakes and white-washed sepulchers full of rotting human bones."

Lucas laughed out loud. He didn't know what life was like in Palestine, but he certainly knew how the priestesses of Diana would accept such criticism. Not at all.

Apollos nodded. "And you're right, young man. Many of these people didn't appreciate it either, but some of them felt really convicted about the things they had done wrong and asked John how they could be forgiven. He called on them all to repent and be baptized and get ready for the coming Messiah. They waded right into the water and John baptized them in the Jordan River. Then they went home to new lives. From then on they tried to be fair and honest and true followers of God and be prepared for the Messiah's arrival. I have been traveling all over preaching this message, and hundreds of people have been baptized and are ready to hear about the Messiah. We have been preaching this for many years. I believe we will hear of Him any day now."

Priscilla clapped her hands together in delight. "This is your day, Apollos. The Messiah has come, and we can tell you all about Him."

"He has?" the preacher exclaimed with delight. "God be praised! This is exciting! Tell me about Him!"

Aquila became the storyteller now. He told how Jesus, the Son of the Israelite's one God, was born in a stable and had His birth announced by angels. Lucas raised an eyebrow. *Certainly interesting,* he thought. He wondered what Diana would think of all this, if she thought at all. Her impassive face on her statues flashed into his mind. While she might be beautiful, her face always seemed cold and expressionless. She seemed to feel the same way all the time. But his mind was wandering, and he turned his attention back to Aquila.

The tentmaker related story after story about Jesus, who had gone around Palestine healing the sick, teaching people how to live better lives, and explaining to them about the kingdom of Jehovah God. It seemed so opposite to the things that went on in the temple of Diana. Even more amazing was the story of how He had so much power and yet allowed the Romans to crucify Him without fighting back. Why would anyone do that? Particularly a god, someone so powerful. It made no sense.

Apparently the look on his face revealed his thoughts, for Aquila stopped. "Lucas," he said, "you have no Jewish background, do you?"

The boy shook his head. His family had had nothing to do with Jews. He considered most of them aloof. And they, of course, had nothing to do with him.

"From the beginning of time," Aquila began, "God's people have loved Him and served Him. But when they sinned, they would bring a lamb, a perfect one, with no blemishes or wounds, and they would sacrifice it to pay for their sins."

Lucas nodded. He was familiar with the concept of offerings.

"The lamb," Aquila continued, "was just pointing forward to the time when the real Lamb of God, our Creator and the Son of God who died for our sins, would finally come. The lamb helped us to anticipate Him. Now that He has come and died, we don't have to sacrifice anymore. We can just pray to Him for forgiveness."

"But if He died—"

"Ah, now we're getting to the good part. He died Friday afternoon."

"But that was the day you said He was crucified," Lucas interrupted. Crucifixions didn't happen very often in Ephesus, but he had seen one. People hung there and suffered and usually died of exposure and dehydration, but it took days.

"Jesus died the same day," Aquila explained. "Some people say He perished from a broken heart. Others say it was the Lord's mercy. And still others say it was because His scourging was so terrible. For whatever reason, He died on Friday. Sunday morning there was a strong earthquake and, even though there was an entire band of Roman soldiers guarding the tomb, an angel rolled the stone away from the entrance and called Jesus forth out of it. The Romans lay around like dead men, unable to move or speak. And Jesus was brought back to life. Lots of people saw Him alive."

"Is He still around?" Lucas asked, fascinated.

Apollos was just as interested.

"No," Aquila said. "He stayed for a short time and spoke to many people, then went back to His Father in heaven. But He sent His Holy Spirit to be with us. Jesus could be in only one place at a time because He had a body like ours, but His Spirit can be everywhere at once and can be with each one of us individually."

"Is His Spirit here now?" Lucas said, glancing around.

"Yes," Priscilla said. "When Aquila and I were baptized, Paul laid hands on us and prayed for the Holy Spirit to come into us, and He did."

"Thank you for telling me all of this," Apollos said, clapping his hands.

Priscilla and Aquila nodded, beaming.

"And thank you," Apollos added, "for bringing me here and telling me privately and not embarrassing me in front of the congregation when I was preaching."

"You were not preaching error," Aquila replied. "Everything you said was right. You just hadn't heard the whole story. Now you have. Jesus never embarrassed anyone on purpose. And as His followers, we try not to either."

As Apollos and Aquila continued talking Lucas looked at Dion. "So this Jesus seems to have come as a normal human being."

"Yes, He looked just like a regular man. What was not ordinary was the way that He treated people and the way that He portrayed God to them."

"That's for sure," Lucas replied. "I can't imagine any of the priestesses or vestal virgins acting the way He did. He seemed to really love people."

"Yes, He did. I think the whole point of Him coming to earth was to reveal what God was like. Everybody was afraid of God, and He seemed so distant that people couldn't understand Him. Jesus wanted to show us what God was like."

"Well that certainly makes sense to me."

The next day as he worked with Demetrius, Lucas told him about the stories he had heard.

"Well," the silversmith said, "this Jesus certainly sounds interesting, but He wouldn't be a great seller as far as statues went."

The boy laughed. "Probably not."

"I'll tell you who's been stirring up things in the marketplace, though," the man continued. "A man named Paul."

"Because of his preaching?"

"Not that. He's been healing sick people and casting out demons."

"Yes, I heard gossip that he was able to do that," Lucas said.

"Well, it's more than that. One day the crowd got so big that they couldn't get the sick people to him. People began bringing handkerchiefs for him to touch, and then they took them home and put them on the sick people and it made them well. It's amazing."

"Really?" the boy said, his eyes widening. "I'd like to see that."

"Well, it's real. I saw it happen, though I don't know how he does it. I sure wish I did. I bet I could earn more money doing that than making these statues of Diana."

Lucas frowned. "I don't think Paul makes much money from it. At least I've heard that he works as a tentmaker when he's not preaching."

Demetrius shook his head. "He may be a good speaker, but he has no sense of business management, or he would be a wealthy man by now."

"I don't think money is his main object in life."

"Well, if it's not, he's just stupid," Demetrius snapped. "That's what life is all about."

The boy said nothing.

The minute Demetrius dismissed him for the afternoon, he hurried toward the marketplace. He hoped Paul would still be there. Maybe he could see someone healed, or perhaps he could follow someone with a handkerchief and watch the healing from a distance. That would be even more amazing.

He was almost to the Agora when he ran into his friend Jason. The boy was one of the few Jews Lucas knew. He had heard that his friend's father claimed to be some kind of a priest.

"Hey, Lucas," Jason called to him. "Where have you been? All kinds of interesting things are happening."

"What kinds of things?"

Jason beckoned him over and with a conspiratorial air whispered in his ear. "We've been watching Paul healing and think we know the secret to it. We're going to try it."

"Who's we?"

"Oh, my brothers and I."

"All seven of you?"

The other boy nodded. "Uh-huh. Do you want to watch?"

"Sure. Does Paul know about this?"

"Of course not," Jason laughed. "I don't think he would like it. But we believe we know the secret. Come on. There's an old demoniac that lives near the gate. He's had these odd fits for years. We're going to try it on him."

"Are you sure Paul won't mind?"

"What difference does it make?" Jason snapped. "He's harmless. Come with us."

Lucas followed his friend back to his home. The other six Sceva sons were waiting.

"We almost left without you, Jason," they said. "Where have you been?"

"Oh, I was talking to my friend Lucas. He wants to join us."

"I have a hunch that soon everyone is going to want to see us performing our miracle," the oldest brother declared.

Lucas felt uncomfortable, but he wasn't sure about what, so he just followed quietly.

When they reached the old man's house, they found him sitting on the ground in a shady spot in front of it, slowly rocking back and forth.

The oldest brother stepped up to him. "Old man, we're going to heal you."

The man glanced up at him and said nothing, but continued to rock back and forth.

All seven boys raised their right hand and chanted together, "In the name of Jesus of Nazareth whom Paul preaches of, we command you to come out of him."

Suddenly the old man leaped to his feet. It seemed like fire flashed from his eyes. With deep, guttural tones that sounded nothing like his normal voice, he shouted, "Jesus I know and Paul I know, but who are you?" He grabbed the oldest one and started punching him viciously.

All of the other six jumped on him to defend their brother. Lucas watched in horror as the old man beat the seven young men unmercifully. He ripped and clawed at their clothes and their skin. Blood spattered as their heads cracked together. It seemed like no time until all seven boys were naked and bleeding.

"Let's get out of here," Jason shouted.

The seven brothers fled from the old man. Lucas was terrified. His feet felt rooted to the ground, and he could do nothing. He closed his eyes. "Jesus of Nazareth whom Paul preaches of," he prayed silently, "please protect me."

The old man turned and stared at Lucas. The boy could taste the fear in his mouth, but he returned the old man's gaze steadily. Slowly the man dropped his fist to his side, shrugged, and walked back to his spot in the shade. There he sat down and resumed his rhythmical rocking.

"Thank You," Lucas whispered, then headed toward home.

This Jesus of Nazareth whom Paul preaches of saved my life, he thought. *And He heard my prayer and answered me. I think I have just become a worshiper.* He drew a deep breath and smiled and changed directions. *I have to go talk to Paul and Dion.*

When he reached Priscilla and Aquila's home, Paul and Dion were sitting in the shade, resting from their day of tent making. They were deep in conversation, so Lucas smiled and sat down next to them, listening intently.

"Have you ever been married?" Dion asked the little man.

Paul nodded. "Yes, in Israel all men are married long before they reach my age. I was too. My wife was from a wealthy family. I was a member of the Sanhedrin and well respected. But when I became a Christian, I became an embarrassment to her, so we divorced, and I have heard that she married a most respectable Levite in Jerusalem."

"I'm never going to marry!" the boy exploded.

Paul smiled. "If you're going to devote your life to the Lord and be a traveling missionary like me or Silas, it's probably easier not to be married, but some people aren't able to do that. And some people miss the physical closeness of a mate, so it's better for them to be married."

Dion frowned. "Yeah, well, I could live the rest of my life without any more of that, too."

"Oh, Dion, what you experienced wasn't love. That was abuse."

Lucas stared at his friend. He had assumed that the boy's life had been easy. After all, he traveled with Paul. But the things the little man was saying now made it sound as if terrible things had happened to Dion back in Corinth. "Did Priscilla and Aquilla do something . . . uh . . . I mean . . . They seem so kind and . . ." His shocked questions faded to an incoherent mumble.

"No! No!" Dion protested. "Priscilla and Aquilla have been wonderful to me. He bought me from a man whom I had been traded to as a way for my real father to pay off my family's debts. My master was . . . well, he did horrible things. I just wanted to die rather than remain with him one more day!"

"Oh," Lucas replied in almost a whisper. "I have heard about those places. That kind of thing happens here, too. I'm so sorry. I had no idea. Here I was feeling sorry for myself and was thinking you had the perfect life, and I was envious."

"Sexual sins can be a problem anywhere," Paul said, "but they seem to be particularly terrible in Corinth. There was a lot of sexual behaviors there that Christians should not do. I'm in the middle of a letter to them about it. Real love between a man and a woman should be gentle and loving. A man should love his wife as Christ loved His church."

Dion shook his head. "That's certainly not how life was between my mother and father."

Paul nodded. "I believe you. But among Christians it should be. Real love is not selfish or cruel, but is patient and kind. It isn't conceited or self-centered.

"You may not ever marry, but if you don't, I hope it is because you are wanting to work for the Lord, and not because you have such terrible memories of warped love."

"Love doesn't look like such a bad thing if it is like the way Priscilla and Aquila seem to love each other," Lucas commented.

His friend slowly nodded.

Paul smiled. "Christians can set an example for everyone else in the world. Or at least they should. Do you know that before Jesus went back to heaven, He told His disciples that the one thing that would make them recognizable to other people anywhere in the world would be the love that they have for each other."

"Really?" Lucas said with surprise.

The little man nodded. "That was more important to Him than what they ate, how they dressed, what day they worshiped on, or any of the other things that His followers are known for."

How wonderful, Lucas thought. *I definitely want to be like that.*

Paul looked up suddenly, as if he was really aware for the first time that Lucas was there. "Lucas, it's good to have you with us."

Dion chuckled. "Paul was so deep in conversation when he was talking to both of us that it hadn't registered that you had joined us."

The missionary sighed. "I guess that's part of getting old."

Lucas shook his head. "You aren't that old. I think it's because you're a lot like my pedagog who took me to school when I was younger and taught me to read. You're so busy thinking about the important things that you just don't notice anything else."

"You're probably right," Paul said. "I think I've always been this way. What's on your mind today?"

Lucas took a deep breath. "I want to be baptized. I have made a decision to become a follower of Jesus Christ."

Paul smiled.

"That's great!" Dion said, then his face clouded. "Do your parents know?"

"No. I came here as soon as I made my choice. But I'm a man now. I can make my own decisions."

"That is right," Paul agreed. "But before you are baptized you need to think about this seriously. Sometimes there are very heavy consequences for the choices we make, even when the choices are good and right."

"I don't care what consequences come from this. Whatever happens happens. I am going to follow the Christ."

"The Lord has a special place in His heart for stubborn young fellows like you," Paul said. "I'm sure your choice is bringing Him great joy."

"May I be baptized now—today?"

"I don't see why not," Paul decided, rising to his feet.

Dion jumped up. "I'll get Priscilla and Aquila. We'll catch up with you. Let's head for the river."

Paul laughed. "Good idea. They won't want to miss this."

* * *

Lucas jolted awake. "My job!" he muttered to himself. "I make graven images. That's not something a Christian can do. What was I thinking?"

He sprang to his feet and pulled on his outer tunic. The sun was just coming up and his parents were still sleeping as he slipped out of their home. Grabbing some bread and cheese, he wandered down the street, munching and muttering to himself.

Paul had been right. Decisions did have consequences. When he had told his parents of his choice, they were not happy with it.

"Nonsense," his father said. "You can't be a follower of this Christ person. That's all there is to it. The entire economy here in Ephesus is based on the worship of Diana. Everyone here earns a living making and selling things either for the temple or to the pilgrims who travel here to worship her. You have no business hanging around with these Christians, and you may not become one. That's all there is to it."

"But—but I am one. I was baptized this afternoon."

"Well, just forget it. Young boys make mistakes. Just consider this one of them. You will go back to work for Demetrius, and I don't want to hear another word about this."

"But I . . ."

"Not another word!" his father exploded.

Lucas didn't know what to do. He had prayed until he fell asleep. "God of Paul and Dion, God of Priscilla and Aquila, please help me to know what to do. My father won't even listen to me, and I'm afraid to say anything more. I have to go to work in the morning, but I can't make more graven images for people to worship. I want people to worship You. Please help me to know what to do." Then he had fallen into a restless sleep.

Nothing seemed much clearer this morning. Suddenly he realized that he had arrived in front of the gate to the silver smithy. "Maybe I can talk to Demetrius about this," he told himself. "He and I have had a lot of conversations. Maybe he will listen to me."

Gathering up his courage—or what was left of it—he walked into the courtyard.

"There you are," Demetrius said. "I'm glad you're here early today."

Lucas nervously smiled. "I came early, because I need to . . ."

"I'm glad you came early," Demetrius said, "because we have a problem here. This Paul person has been doing way too much preaching here in our city. At first I thought he was harmless, but he's not. Do you know that the people who have listened to him are getting rid of their statues of Diana? Not only that, but they are spreading the word to other people. Worship at the temple is way down, as are offerings. And we still have a whole bunch of statues left over from the past two days. They're not selling well.

"Our friend down the street who sells the books of magic and spells says not only that the demand for them has fallen off, but that he has heard that people had a bonfire last night at which a bunch of these believers or whatever they call themselves brought their books and burned them in the public square. Can you imagine? We've talked it over, and we just can't have this. The entire economy of this city is built around the worship of Diana. This Paul seemed harmless in the beginning, but he's going to ruin Ephesus. We won't be able to make a living. And not only that—we won't have the travelers coming here. This Christianity stuff is spreading everywhere. Everyone who makes a living feeding and housing the tourists and selling things to them will be unable to support their families. All of us will starve because of this Paul person's God."

"That's what I needed to talk to you about," Lucas started again, but Demetrius interrupted him.

"I've talked to some other people, and we are going to gather later this morning in the town square. I want you to round up as many of your friends as you can and show up. I'll give a silver coin to everyone who comes and participates. I need a lot of you young men with strong voices."

"Why? What are we going to do?"

"We're going to protest and drive this Paul character out of town."

"I can't be part of that," Lucas said slowly.

"Of course you can," Demetrius replied. "Now go get your friends. And don't come back without them. We need as large a crowd as we can get."

"But, but," he protested.

"Out you go," the man said, shoving him out the gate. "Go on, you know what you're supposed to do. Get on with it—I can't stand around talking all day."

Lucas walked down the street. "Jehovah God," he whispered, "God of Paul and Priscilla and Aquila, and Jesus, whom I've given my life to, what can I do?" Frustration welled up inside him. "I just don't know what to do."

Suddenly he realized what he needed to do right then, even if he couldn't figure out the rest of it. Someone needed to warn Paul. He turned and ran toward the house of Aquila.

* * *

Lucas watched from the edge of the crowd. The huge mob filled the entire city square and marketplace. Demetrius had worked them into a frenzy as they all shouted, "Great is Diana of the Ephesians! Great is Diana of the Ephesians!" He noticed that many people seemed to have no idea what they were protesting but were just going along with the rest. Some of their slogans even contradicted each other. Though the excitement was contagious, Lucas stood with his arms folded across his chest in silence. Other believers had kept Paul from coming to the city square to address the mob. He didn't think anyone could speak to the frenzied crowd. He wondered if anyone could talk sense to them. Perhaps someone, but not Paul.

Finally the town clerk stepped up onto the bema, or platform. "Fellow citizens," he shouted.

Somehow the mob quieted a little. Lucas shook his head. If they hadn't listened to Alexander, one of the believers who had tried to speak to them, would they pay any attention to the town clerk?

Then suddenly things settled down. Maybe they would listen.

"Fellow citizens," he shouted again, "is there anyone anywhere who doesn't know that our dear city Ephesus is the protector of glorious Artemis and her sacred stone image that fell straight out of heaven? Since this is beyond contradiction, you had better get hold of yourselves. Such conduct is unworthy of Artemis. These men you've dragged in here have done nothing to harm either our temple or our goddess" (Acts 19:35-37, Message).

A murmur rippled through the crowd.

"If Demetrius and his guild of artisans have a complaint," the official continued, "they can take it to court and make all the accusations they want to. And if anything else is bothering you, you need to bring it to the regularly scheduled town meeting and let it be settled there. There's no excuse for what's happened today. Besides that, the Romans take a very dim view of this kind of behavior. We're putting our city in serious danger. Remember, the Empire doesn't look kindly on rioters."

The crowd's response grew louder.

"I suggest you all go home and think about this."

To Lucas's amazement, the crowd broke up, and people slipped off quietly. What had been a screaming mass of angry people suddenly melted into a few knots of men talking quietly among themselves.

"Oh, thank You, God," Lucas whispered. He headed toward home, wondering if his father had been in the crowd. He hadn't seen him, but he wasn't sure.

When he walked in the door, his father met him. "Where were you today?"

"In the Agora," Lucas answered truthfully.

"Well, that's not what Demetrius told me. He said you were supposed to come back here and gather some friends and meet him there. You didn't do that. I saw you standing off to the side, not even participating in the demonstration."

"That's true. But those involved in it were reprimanded and sent home, so I thought it was all right just to watch."

"It's not all right," his father exploded. "You work for Demetrius. Well, at least you did. But you don't anymore. If you're not going to support him and his business and do the things he asks you to, there are plenty of other young people who will. He doesn't want you to come back again. And you can forget this week's wages."

Not sure how to respond, Lucas swallowed hard. He had prayed for a way to get out of his job, but being fired didn't feel good either.

"Furthermore," his father continued, "you are a terrible embarrassment to the family. Are you still planning to follow this Paul person?"

His son slowly nodded. "I have been baptized as a follower of Jesus Christ."

"Well, as long as you feel that way, you are no longer my son. Get out of my house and don't ever come back." And with that he pushed his son out and slammed the door.

The boy stood there stunned. What would he do now? He had no place to stay. No money. No belongings. No job. "Are You seeing this, God?" he whispered. "Do You know what I should do next?" Then, as he had done so many times that week, he turned and walked toward the house of Aquila. Perhaps Paul would have a suggestion.

* * *

Lucas stretched and yawned. "Are you tired?" his friend Eutychus asked.

"Not really," Lucas replied. "Paul spent most of today dictating, and I'm not used to sitting for so long."

Eutychus laughed. "If I had to sit all day and write things, I would just hate it."

"I don't mind that much. Traveling with Paul has been fun, and I didn't have a lot of other options at the time, so I was glad that I know how to write."

"I bet you've been to a lot of interesting places," Eutychus commented.

Lucas nodded. "When we left Ephesus, we went to Macedonia, and Paul visited places he had been before. It was like a family reunion at each town where he had started a church. Also we went to Corinth, which was really interesting. My friend Dion had come from there and had told me so many things about it. It was interesting to see the places he had talked about and meet the people I had heard stories about."

"Does Paul have you write a lot?"

"It depends. Sometimes we're traveling; sometimes he's busy preaching. And he does not accept money from any of the congregations for his own needs, so we spend some time tentmaking. But we have written some really long letters. For example, he sent one to the Galatians since he had started several groups in Galatia and had heard some disturbing things about them."

"Like what?"

"Well, when they were baptized in the name of Jesus Christ, they were delivered from all of the rigid rules the Jews had imposed on themselves to be good enough to please God. Then new teachers told the people that they still had to keep this rule and that rule. The people there became confused since they wanted to please God and were afraid to make Him angry, so they did what the new teachers told them. Paul wrote to them that they didn't need to be so afraid."

"Does he write only to the churches he started?" Eutychus questioned.

"Oh, no. One of the letters we finished recently was to the church in Rome."

"Paul hasn't been to Rome. I heard my father say that. How could there be a church there?"

"There are a lot of Christians around now. The faith is spreading throughout the whole world. And there is a church in Rome. Paul wants to visit them, but I'm not sure we're going there next. He's been talking about returning to Jerusalem before he visits Rome."

"Really?" Eutychus said in disbelief. "Why would he go there? That's the most dangerous place in the world for him. The Jewish leaders hate him."

"I know. I don't understand it exactly. But there are a lot of times when the way Paul thinks doesn't make much sense to me. But he's interesting to travel with, and I really like acting as his scribe. I've learned a lot."

"If you say so."

"Well," Lucas continued, "I need to eat some supper now if I'm going to get any before the preaching tonight. This is Paul's last night here, so it could go on a long time."

Eutychus sighed. "I know what you mean. Let's find some food. My mother probably has something ready."

The two boys headed for the home of Eutychus.

The evening meeting had already lasted for some time when Paul paused in his preaching. Suddenly someone stood up and waited to be recognized. Lucas glanced at Eutychus and raised an eyebrow.

"It's Agabus," his friend whispered with a yawn. "He's a prophet."

By now Agabus had pulled off his belt from around his waist and tied it around Paul's hands. "If you go back to Jerusalem," the prophet said, "your hands will be tied just like this and you will be imprisoned."

Eutychus's father jumped to his feet. "Paul, you must not go."

The whole group began to speak at once, everyone giving their opinion on what Paul should or should not do.

Finally the apostle raised his hands. "Stop! Stop! I understand that my mission may be coming to an end. However, I need to go back to Jerusalem whether or not I'm arrested."

"Then is this the last time we will see you?" one of the women in the front of the group asked Paul.

Paul sighed. "I believe it might be."

Tears began to glisten in many eyes. Lucas felt a knot forming in his stomach. *What about me?* he wondered. *God, are You watching? Do You see this?*

I smiled and drew closer to the young man. If only these humans could understand. Yes, the Mighty One is always watching. And yes, He has plans and backup plans and more plans and resources that would stagger the mind of His fearful human worshipers.

Everybody settled down now as Paul began giving his final words of advice to the group of Christians he had started years before.

The boys slipped over to the far side of the room where they could talk softly without causing a distraction.

"Hey, Lucas," Eutychus whispered, "if you and Paul go back to Jerusalem, and Paul's going to be arrested, what will happen to you?"

"I don't know."

"It would be hard for you to take care of yourself in a place like that. You're not a Jew and don't know anybody there. What would you do?"

"I don't know," Lucas repeated. "But I do know that God has taken care of me even when it looked as if my whole world was falling apart in Ephesus. I guess He'll have to take care of me again."

"I wish I had as much faith as you did. You always seem so strong. It must be from traveling with Paul."

Lucas smiled. "Not that strong. I'm scared too. But once you make a commitment and start following God, you have no choice but to continue trusting Him. There's no going back, and I don't think I'd want to even if I could."

Suddenly Eutychus yawned again. "It is so stuffy in here. I'm sweating like a farmhand."

"Me too."

"These stone windowsills are pretty wide. Let's sit up here. Then we can catch the night breezes and still hear what's going on."

"Good idea," Lucas agreed. The two boys climbed up and sat in the wide window toe to toe with their backs leaning against the sides.

It seemed as if Paul had been preaching forever. Although Lucas tried to stay awake, he kept feeling his head drooping. He would jerk it back up and try to force his eyes to stay open.

Suddenly he heard a sickening thud. Lucas snapped awake to realize that Eutychus had fallen from the window. As he looked down to the stone-paved street below and saw his friend lying motionless it felt as if a giant vise was crushing his chest.

Pandemonium broke out as people realized what had happened. First they rushed to the window, then for the stairs. Lucas remained, as if paralyzed, in the window. As the people gathered around Eutychus's body, the women began to wail. Lucas's worst fears had come true. His friend Eutychus was dead.

I shook my head at the human sadness. The guardians had been present, yet they had held back on command as the youth had fallen out the window. The Almighty did not always allow them to intervene. Bad things happened to good people, too. It was part of the horrible results of sin.

"Back up! Let Paul through. Paul wants to see." The little knot of people parted to allow him to reach the boy's side.

"He's dead," one believer gasped. "Look at the angle his head is at. I'm sure his neck is broken."

They rolled the boy over onto his back. Blood trickled from his nose and ears. He was not breathing.

Suddenly Paul dropped to his knees and began praying. Then he seemed to be covering the boy's body with his own.

I started with joy as I saw the bolt of energy cleave the heavens and shoot down into the dead youth lying on the pavement. It was the touch of the Mighty One Himself.

The boy coughed and began to move. Paul stood and then lifted Eutychus to his feet.

"He's alive! He's alive!" the crowd exclaimed.

"Thank you, Paul, thank you," the lad's mother cried.

The apostle shook his head. "No; thank God."

The group hurried inside and started a meeting of praise and thanks to God for bringing life back into Eutychus. The boy seemed a bit dazed and embarrassed, but very much alive.

Lucas just stared. Only a short time ago he and Eutychus had been talking about trusting God to take care of them. Then the Lord had reached down and showed them that He could fix *anything*. Even death was not a complication He couldn't handle. After drawing a deep breath, Lucas smiled. If God could raise to life a dead person, certainly He could take care of a live one. It did not matter if Paul was arrested in Jerusalem.

As Lucas watched, Eutychus's parents whispered quietly to each other. Then Eutychus's father approached Paul.

"We love you," he said. "You have been our teacher and our father as we have learned to grow in Christ. And you prayed for our son so that he was restored to us. While we don't know what to give you or to do for you to show how much we appreciate you, we would like to do something for the young man who's been traveling with you."

"What do you have in mind?" the missionary asked.

"If you're returning to Jerusalem where your life is going to be in danger, would you consider allowing the lad to stay and live with us? We never had any more children after Eutychus was born. If you would let him remain, we would love to keep Lucas and treat him as our own son."

Paul rubbed his chin thoughtfully. "It's true that I travel to some dangerous places, and I don't know what could happen to the lad . . ." He paused, not needing to finish the rest of his sentence. Then he glanced over at Lucas. "How do you feel? Would you like to stay here in Troas and become part of your friend Eutychus's family?"

Stunned, the boy nodded. "I—I would. You've been good to me, and I have loved traveling with you, but if Agabus is right . . ."

"Of course Agabus is right," Paul said simply.

Lucas stared at his feet.

"Very well, then. Lucas, I'm giving you to this family." He turned to Eutychus's parents. "This young man is my gift to you. Love him and care for him and treat him well, for he's precious to me."

"We will," they solemnly replied.

Lucas glanced over at Eutychus. His friend grinned back. "I guess that makes us brothers," he said.

"I guess it does. I told you the Lord could take care of things."

Eutychus reached up and rubbed his head. "Yes, He certainly did. I just wish it all didn't have to be quite so dramatic."

"Well, it never has to be again as long as you stay awake in church from now on."

And I smiled too. Once again the Mighty One showed His love for these fragile people and His ability to take care of them.

Matteo

(Mediterranean Sea)

atteo drew in a deep breath of the salty sea air and smiled. He loved the sea. Ever since he could remember he had wanted to sail with his father who owned his own ship. Now Father had finally decided he was old enough to go along, and the boy loved it. The rest of the crew treated him well because he was the son of the captain. And he was learning quickly.

I smiled too. While he was a new assignment, I had still arrived early enough to hear the negotiations between his father and Julius, a centurion of the elite guard who just happened to have Paul, the great preacher, in his custody. It was going to be an eventful trip.

The boy was excited. He had been several places since he had joined his father on the ship. But he hadn't been to Rome, and that was where they were headed.

Matteo had enjoyed the time they had spent in Lycia while the ship unloaded passengers and merchandise and replenished their water and food supplies. But Rome was the place everyone talked about. He couldn't wait to see it.

The final afternoon before leaving, the centurion, with a few soldiers and their prisoner, boarded the ship. Two other prisoners were already chained to the wall in the cargo hold below, so this was not unusual. What was unusual was the polite manner the military officer treated his charge.

At his father's request Matteo had followed them down and shown them where soldiers and prisoners would spend the trip. He then brought fresh water to the three prisoners. One prisoner refused to speak to him, but drank the water. The second one spit in the cup and cursed the boy. Matteo had learned to stand out of this prisoner's reach. His father had warned him about the danger. The boy had no idea that the guardians stood between him and the angry prisoner, protecting him.

"Easy there," the new centurion said to the belligerent prisoner. "You can act however you want to to us soldiers. But if you had any sense at all, you'd be nice to the boy. He's the one that's going to provide you food and water. And if you're going to act like that, you won't be getting any more."

The prisoner glared at the officer. "What difference would that make? Does it matter whether I die here in the ship's hold or when I get to Rome?"

The centurion shrugged. "No, it doesn't matter to me, but you won't be treating the child that way."

Matteo pulled himself up as tall as he could. He didn't like being called a child. Turning to the new prisoner, he offered him water.

The man thanked him.

Surprised, Matteo stammered, "Uh, you're welcome." He wasn't used to prisoners being polite.

"My name is Paul," the prisoner said. "And you are?"

"Matteo."

"Well, it's good to meet you, Matteo. I guess we'll be seeing a lot of each other on this voyage."

"I guess so." He hurried back on deck.

"Matteo," his dad called when he saw him, "check on the prisoners downstairs and see that they have fresh water."

"I just did. Everyone who wanted any has had water."

"The belligerent one, huh?"

"Yes, and he wouldnt' drink anything. He just cursed and spat again."

His father shrugged. "Whatever makes him happy. What about the new prisoner?"

"He's really different."

The boy's father laughed bitterly. "Well, they're all really different."

"No, this one is polite, and the centurion with him treats him with respect."

Another shrug. "If they're in chains in the hold of the ship, they're criminals. They're all the same. If the centurion is being polite to him and he acts as if he has manners, it'll make the trip more pleasant for us. But they're all the same—trust me. He probably just has important connections and so the centurion is being careful with him."

I almost laughed out loud. If only he knew whom Paul had a connection with. And then I paused to think a moment. Actually, the captain was right in one respect. It was Paul's connection with someone higher up that had made it possible for him to be treated so respectfully by the feared Roman guards.

They were just getting ready to sail out of the harbor when the prisoner spoke. "I must speak with the captain," he said. "It's urgent!"

The centurion turned and called to Matteo. "Young man."

"Yes, sir," the boy answered respectfully.

"The prisoner here wishes to speak to your father, the captain."

"I'll let him know right away."

Matteo scrambled up the ladder to the upper deck as quick as a monkey and ran to his father. "The new prisoner needs to speak to you right away."

"I'll bet he does," his father grimaced.

"No, really. The centurion asked me to fetch you."

"The centurion did? Of all the things I have to do, coddling the prisoners is not one of them. That's his job." His father grumbled all the way across the deck and down the ladder, then stood silently before the prisoner.

"You are the captain?" Paul asked politely.

The boy's father nodded.

"It would be better for us to stay here through the winter."

The captain father laughed. "This is what you called me down here to say?"

Paul inclined his head.

"I have work to do." He turned on his heel and left.

"It is late in the season," Paul said to his retreating back. "This is not a good time to be making a journey by ship. We will have severe weather."

After the captain left, Julian the centurion shrugged. "You did your best to warn him."

As they sailed away the weather seemed fine. However, that evening black clouds rolled in. It began to rain, and soon the wind blew too hard to leave the sails up.

"Pull them down," the captain shouted to the crew. "We don't want them ripped to shreds."

The rain continued for days. They sailed into a place called Good Harbor on the island of Crete. The crew seemed relieved and made a lot of puns about what a good harbor Good Harbor was.

Paul asked to see the captain again. Although Matteo's father rolled his eyes, he climbed down into the hold.

"I see only disaster ahead for the cargo and the ship, to say nothing of our lives," Paul warned. "If we put out to sea now, we'll be in terrible trouble."

"Look, I am the captain of this ship. I am the one that makes the decisions. You are a prisoner. Even if it is wintertime and the weather is not as good as in the summer, this is not the best harbor to stay in, no matter what they named it. There's a better one a few miles further on, and if we do have to hole up for the winter, I'd rather stay there." He abruptly departed.

"Please," Paul urged the centurion, "please talk to him. Our lives are in danger."

"I'll try," Julian sighed. He followed the captain up on deck.

Confused, Matteo hurried along behind him to hear what the soldier would say. Paul had sounded serious. The boy really wished his father would stay in the harbor. Yet he knew his father had been sailing all his adult life. Matteo was certain he knew what he was doing.

His father and the centurion talked for a few moments; then the centurion went back down to Paul. The crew pulled up the anchor, and they sailed out of Good Harbor.

It seemed only a short time before the black clouds rolled in again. This time the storm was even worse. Matteo had been pretty confident that his father knew what he was doing, yet now as he clung desperately to the mast, he felt as if the ship was a tiny cork on the ocean. The waves crashed onto the deck, knocking anything or anyone loose across it.

His father staggered toward him. "Get off the deck," he shouted above the wind and waves. "Go below. It's too dangerous up here. We've already lost one sailor overboard. At least I think that's what happened to him. Go below. You'll be safer there."

However, down below deck didn't feel any safer. In the darkness he clung miserably to the ladder. This was one time when the men chained to the wall seemed to have it better than anyone else. At least they didn't get thrown back and forth as much, though Matteo doubted if they were comfortable.

It seemed like hours before his father precariously stumbled down the ladder. "We're near an island," he shouted. "Now we're going to ready the ship's boat and get at least some of us ashore."

Matteo wondered how many people the ship's boat could actually take to shore and whether he would rather be in the hold of this ship being tossed back and forth and smacked into the walls or whether he wanted to be in a little open boat on the waves. Neither choice was very appealing.

I hovered close, as was my duty. But it was comforting to see the guardians surrounding the ship. The ship may have appeared to be out of control, but with such a tight ring of guardians nothing could happen to it that wasn't planned. Unfortunately, none of the humans could see them, and most of the passengers and crew were terrified. At least those who were not too seasick to think about it.

Matteo waited and waited, yet his father never came back. Surely they had gotten the ship's boat into the water by now. Finally he climbed up to see what was happening. It seemed to take forever to get across the deck to where his father was.

"What are you doing up here?" the captain shouted above the screaming wind.

"Where is the ship's boat?" the boy asked. "I thought you forgot me."

His father put his arm around him. "I didn't forget you, son. There were too many rocks around this island. We couldn't get close enough. If we had lowered the ship's boat, it would have smashed to pieces on the rocks. Only by throwing out our sea anchors have we barely avoided getting smashed on the rocks ourselves. Now we have gone back out to deeper water and will just have to weather this out. We aren't near anyplace that we can put in for shelter."

The boy's heart sank. He tried to say something, but his voice wouldn't work. The deck seemed to leap up at him and then plunge into the depths of the sea. He bent over and threw up. His father pulled him by the arm across the deck. "Come on; you can't stay up here. Go below and be miserable with the other passengers."

Shakily Matteo lowered himself down the ladder and huddled in one corner of the cargo hold, hanging on for dear life. It was dark in the hold, and as the hours ran together he couldn't tell if it was day or night.

Finally his father slid down the ladder and announced, "We're going to have to dump the cargo if we want to survive this. Everyone give me a hand."

The soldiers and passengers formed a line passing the heavy sacks and jars of grain from one to another and up to the top deck. When all the cargo had been moved, everyone settled back down to pray for calm water.

The misery went on and on. Matteo awoke to his father bending over him and giving him a sip of water.

"Come on, son, drink this. It doesn't seem right in all this water for a person to die of thirst. Now swallow."

Matteo did his best to get the water down, but his stomach rebelled. "Is it any better up there?" he asked.

His father shook his head. "It's been three days now, and I had the crew throw off all of our tackle and all the food and provisions."

"How far are we from land?"

"I have no idea. It's been so many days since we've seen the sun or any stars, who knows what direction we're drifting."

"You threw all the food overboard? How are we going to survive?"

His father laughed bitterly. "Does it matter? You don't look hungry anyway."

Matteo shook his head. "I'm not. I can't eat."

"Friends," Paul said from the darkness, "you really should have listened to me when we were back in Crete. Then we wouldn't be in all this trouble now."

The boy's father glared at where he thought the prisoner must be sitting.

"I suppose there's no need to labor that point," Paul continued. "But cheer up; things are looking better. Not a single one of us is going to drown, although the ship isn't going to survive."

"How do you know this?" Matteo's father demanded.

"An angel told me. Last night an angel stood at my side and said, 'Paul, don't worry. You're going to make it to Rome and stand before Caesar just as you've asked, and everyone sailing with you is going to survive too.' So cheer up, friends, God will do exactly as He said. But I'm afraid we are going to be shipwrecked."

"Did your God happen to tell you what island we were going to land on?" the captain asked sarcastically.

Paul didn't answer him.

Matteo felt too miserable to care.

On the fourteenth night the storm continued, but somehow things felt different. The boy's father came below deck.

"Come on, son, I'm taking you topside."

Matteo opened his eyes. "Is the storm over?" he asked, his voice raspy.

"No, but I'd feel better with you up near me."

The rest of the crew, the passengers, and the prisoners crawled up on deck too.

The boy listened as they dropped the sounding rope over the side of the ship.

"It's 120 feet deep," a crew member said, and then, "Now it's 90 feet deep. It's getting shallow quickly."

"Let's throw some anchors out. We don't want to run aground in the dark here. After daylight we'll try to figure out what to do."

Matteo noticed two sailors whispering together. "The anchor is near the ship's boat," one said. "We can drop it, then lower the boat and escape to shore."

The boy frantically glanced around, but his father wasn't anywhere in sight. He tried to stand, but collapsed back down on the deck.

At that moment Paul pointed to the two men and announced, "If those sailors don't stay with the ship, we'll all go down. We have to stay together."

Quickly Julian and his soldiers leaped toward the sailors. They had the ship's boat lowered only halfway when the soldiers grabbed them. With a slash of their short swords they cut the ropes holding the lifeboat. It plunged into the water and vanished in the waves.

"We are all going to do this together," Julian declared.

The sailors said nothing.

The next time the centurion opened his eyes he noticed a faint glow on the horizon. It was almost morning.

"Friends," Paul shouted, "listen to me. You've gone without food for 14 days. So have I. Who felt like eating? But now you must— you will need your strength. We are going to be shipwrecked today, and you're going to need to be strong enough to swim. Cheer up. We're all going to make it out of this alive. Is there any food left?"

"Yes, a little," Matteo's father replied. "That big basket in the storage room has some dried figs."

"Good. Get it."

Two sailors carried the basket out. Paul said a prayer and then started tearing the fig cakes into individual servings and passing them around.

Matteo glanced around him. Altogether the ship had carried 276 people when they had left the harbor. It looked as if everyone was still there. The sailor whom his father thought had been swept overboard was still with them.

"You need to eat too," his father urged.

The boy shook his head. "I can't."

"Yes, you can. This prisoner has been right about everything else so far, so he's probably right about this. You must eat."

When Matteo did, amazingly the food stayed down.

As the light spread through the sky they were able to see the island they skirted, but no one recognized it. However, farther down the coast they spotted a bay with a nice beach.

"Can we make it to shore?" one of the sailors asked.

Matteo's father nodded. "I think so. If we cut the anchors, loosen the steering oar, and raise one sail, we should be able to catch the wind and go straight for the beach. If we run aground there, we should all be fine."

The sailors nodded. Everyone ran to their post. But with the storm still howling around them and the rain pelting in their faces, things didn't work the way they were supposed to. With a shudder and a snapping of timbers the ship hit a rock and began to break up.

The soldiers quickly unsheathed their swords. If any prisoners escaped, they would have to pay with their lives. It was much easier just to kill them and be done with it.

"No," Julian ordered, "we're not going to do that this time." He turned to the others on deck. "Now I'm giving the orders here. Anyone who can swim, dive in and go. The rest of you come to this end of the ship." The vessel was breaking up rapidly. "If you can't swim, grab on to one of these planks, then kick with your legs and get to the beach as quickly as you can."

*　*　*

Matteo looked around. The boy couldn't believe he was finally on land. But it didn't feel solid. The ground seemed to be rising and falling, as if he were still on the deck of the ship. But his father said that it was all an illusion in his head and that it would fade away. He lay on the ground near a fire. The people from the island had built them a huge roaring fire. They had even brought some food. As Matteo watched, several of the sailors, and even Paul, helped carry more sticks to throw on the fire.

Suddenly the boy's heart froze. Although he pointed and tried to shout, nothing would come out of his mouth. It was just like the nightmares he had had when he was younger. A venomous snake curled up around the sticks that Paul was carrying. The apostle didn't seem to notice. Then quick as lightning the serpent struck, and sank its fangs into his hand. Everyone jumped back.

One person near Matteo said, "Obviously he was a murderer. He may have survived the shipwreck, but the gods aren't going to let him get away."

Paul turned around and looked him straight in the eye. "No," he said, "my God is going to take care of all of us. Even me." He shook his hand. The snake dropped off into the fire. Everyone sat in silence watching him. The venom of such snakes took only minutes to kill their victims. But although they waited for Paul to drop dead, nothing happened.

Matteo sat up. The sense of rocking up and down was starting to go away, and Paul was obviously feeling fine. The boy crept over next to him. "Your God really did take care of you, didn't He?"

"I told you He would."

"Will you tell me more about Him?"

"Absolutely," Paul replied.

Just then a tall, well-dressed man approached. "My name is Publius. I would be honored if you would be guests in my home."

Matteo and his father, Julian and Paul, and two other soldiers returned with Publius to his home. It felt so good to be inside a real house, to sleep under comfortable blankets on a mat that didn't throw him back and forth. Soon the boy felt like his old self. However, not everyone was well in the house. Their host's father had a high fever and dysentery.

"May I see him?" Paul asked.

Publius led him into the older man's room. The apostle knelt, laid his hands on him, and prayed. The father was healed.

Somehow Matteo was not surprised at what happened. He had listened to three days of stories about Paul's God. If He could raise a dead youth back to life, then a little case of diarrhea certainly was nothing that He couldn't handle.

* * *

Paul raised his hand above Matteo's hand. "I baptize you in the name of the Father and His Son, Jesus, and His Holy Spirit, our Comforter," he said, lowered the boy into the water, then pulled him back up. After hugging him, the apostle announced, "Now you are a follower of Christ. We are brothers."

Matteo beamed. "I just wish we could finish this journey together."

"I know. So do I. But I believe our paths will cross again someday. Just remember everything that I have taught you in the past three months. Share it with anyone who will listen, and be patient with your father. He is a good man in his heart, and the Holy Spirit will work with him. Just be respectful and obedient to him, and when he asks, then tell him these things."

The boy nodded. "I will." He smiled at the centurion, who stood dripping on the bank. "Is it going to make it hard for you to be both a Christian and a soldier?"

Julian shrugged. "I don't know. I've never been a Christian before. I guess I'll find out soon enough. We are brothers too. I hope we meet again. Perhaps we will someday. The elite guard does get around."

The Mighty One had brought these men together and, though they had been through a terrible ordeal, had kept them all safe and held them close to His heart, where they couldn't help responding to His love. I took a deep breath and smiled. I love my job. Even more than that, I love the One I work for.

Vesta

(aboard a ship en route to Rome)

esta drew in a deep breath of the cool sea air as she walked carefully along the deck. Matteo, her new husband, wanted her to stay in the cramped cabin in the hull as much as possible, but she just couldn't stand it anymore. Never designed for passengers, it was just a tiny place where the captain could sleep in safety and lock any personal valuables from the other crew or occasional passengers who slept anywhere they could in the dank hold of the ship.

"A ship is no place for women," he had said. "But I am taking you home, and Rome is a long way to swim from here." Vesta smiled. Her father had been concerned about the trip too, though she wasn't sure if it was because of the sea voyage or that he was saying goodbye to his only daughter.

It was important to both Vesta and her parents that she marry a believer. But when Matteo had asked to take her as his wife, her mother and father found it hard to let her go. "I know that he will treat you well and that you will be happy," her mother sobbed. "It's just that Rome is so far away." If it hadn't been that Paul was a friend of the young sailor, they might not have been willing to part with her.

When Matteo noticed his pretty young wife standing at the rail, he hurried over to her.

"I'm sorry," she said as he approached. "I just can't stay in there anymore. I had to come up for some air."

"I understand," he replied. "The trip is too long to ask anyone who isn't in chains to remain below. Just please be extremely careful. I'm not sure whom I trust less—the crew or the passengers. I just want you to be safe."

"Really? The only people I have seen so far look harmless. I've spent my whole life around bad people, and no one aboard looks as scary as the ones who came through my father's jail in Philippi."

"Looks can be deceiving, my love," he murmured quietly. "See that man over there? I believe he is a runaway slave. The hole in his ear could have held a slave ring, but there is nothing in it now. If it contained a temple jewel to his goddess or some other decoration, he would still have it in, and there would be one in each ear."

"Oh," she replied quietly. "Escaping slaves can be desperate people." She shuddered as she remembered the treatment that they had received when they had been caught and held in jail till their owners picked them up. Their owners could do anything to them, even beat them to death. Nobody could interfere, and slaves had no rights at all. No wonder they were desperate.

"What about the other passengers?" she asked.

"There is a pair of men traveling together from Ephesus. Though they keep to themselves, they seem harmless enough. Another two boarded in Ephesus too, but say they are from Lystra. I don't believe them, though. One is definitely a Jew; the other one I'm not sure about. He speaks good Greek, however. They always seem to have a papyrus roll in their hands. At least they are only reading. Another Jew who is horribly seasick and probably down below throwing up even as we speak also spends his time with papyrus and keeps scribbling. I don't think he is a writer, though—he doesn't look important enough. I think he is probably just a scribe trying to get the document copied before he gets to his destination for whoever his employer is. I'm so glad you don't get seasick!"

"Me too! This would be a horribly long trip if I had to remain closed up in that little room and seasick too! Aren't there any other women on this ship?"

"Not usually," her husband said, "but this time we have one besides you."

"Oh, good! Would it be all right if I talk with her?"

"She is with the one who looks like an escapee. Always wears those heavy dark veils so I don't know what she really looks like. And she might be dangerous, too."

"Oh, Matteo, I'll be careful."

"If anyone bothers you, yell and scream a lot. I have things I have to do, but I will be around and will keep my ears and eyes open." He looked at her puffy eyes. Though she had never complained to him, he knew she was homesick. Perhaps getting out on deck and even talking to the other woman passenger would be good for her and get her mind off missing her parents. "It's only for a little while," he whispered to her. "You will love your new home. We live outside of Rome away from the crowding and the city smells. The estate has terraced vineyards and trees and beautiful gardens. My parents are believers too, as are most of our household servants."

Vesta smiled, though her chin trembled a little. "I know. I am so fortunate to have been given a husband who is marrying me for love and one who is a believer, too. God has been good to me. I know it will be all right. Its just that . . . I . . . um . . ." A tear escaped before she could stop it. She looked away, hoping he hadn't seen it.

He had seen it but wasn't sure what to do about it. After all, he'd never had a wife before. Seeing a woman he loved in tears made him feel as helpless as a shipwreck. "I need to take care of some things before the crew decide I am a softheaded lovesick boy," he whispered. "Call if you need me."

As Vesta gazed over the rippling water she felt her spirits lifting. God didn't feel quite so far away out here. Now she stood quietly whispering to him. It had been several years since she had first fallen in love with Paul's God. Remembering that night when the earthquake had broken the prison open and her father had stood with his sword to his chest, she shuddered. The apostle had kept him from committing suicide. And her family's life had changed that night. They had all become believers and helped form the nucleus of a new group that had grown rapidly. Her whole family adored Paul.

A shadow fell across the deck as the woman from below approached the rail. Glancing at her, Vesta smiled. The other woman had covered herself so that only her eyes showed. Vesta thought she had the saddest eyes she had ever seen.

"I am Vesta of Philippi," she said. "Well, I was Vesta of Phillipi. Now I am married to Matteo, so I guess I am Vesta of . . . of . . . I forgot the name of the place he lives, but it is a little way from Rome."

"I am Cassandra," the veiled woman replied. "I am not really from anywhere. I've lived a lot of places. We are going to someplace near Rome too. You are married to the captain of the ship?"

"Yes, well, no. Yes, we are married. We just got married, and Matteo is taking me home to his family. He isn't really the captain of the ship, though. Well, he is right now, but his father owns the ships, two of them. Matteo and his brothers and his father work together, but it all belongs to his father."

"Congratulations on your wedding. I hope your married life is happy and fruitful," the woman said in a sad voice. "I thought he looked pretty young to be a captain of a ship."

"Are you married?"

"I was once. A long time ago."

The young man with the empty hole in his earlobe approached

them. "This is my son Onesimus," the woman said with the first trace of happiness.

"Mother, it is better if you stay with me," he said quietly.

"Oh, don't worry," Vesta protested. "My husband won't let anything happen to us up here. And I won't tell anybody who you are."

"Oh?" He raised a dark eyebrow. "And what is it you won't tell?"

"That you are Onesimus and . . . well . . . I wouldn't tell anything else. I wouldn't want you to get caught or anything."

"See, Mother?" he whispered. "It is dangerous for you to talk with anyone."

"I would never do you any harm!" Vesta said angrily. "I know what they do to runaway slaves, and I would never be a part of hurting anyone like that."

"That's just the point," Onesimus retorted. "I am not a runaway slave. I am a freedman, and I have manumission papers for my mother, too. But when nosy people get an idea in their heads it doesn't matter what it says on your documents. Sometimes people beat you first and then look at your papers afterward." He turned back to his mother. "Please stay with me and don't talk to anyone else till we get to Paul's friends. Then you will be safe and can chat with anyone you want to. I promise."

"Paul?" Vesta echoed. "Do you mean Paul of Tarsus? Paul the believer? Paul the great preacher? Paul who has been in prison in Rome? That Paul?"

The two turned to Vesta in surprise. "You know him?" they asked together.

"We love Paul!" she exclaimed joyfully. "He kept my father from having to commit suicide in Philippi when an earthquake broke the jail open. Then he taught our family about Yeshua and baptized all of us. Later he told Matteo and his father about my family, and he is the reason my family felt safe giving me to Matteo as a bride."

"You are the jailer's daughter from Philippi?" asked Onesimus' mother. "We've heard about you. Your father has helped grow a whole crop of believers in Philippi."

"Yes, that is true," Vesta answered. "But how do you know Paul?"

"I was a slave," the man said. "Mother and I were both slaves of a man named Philemon. Philemon became a believer a couple years ago. I escaped. He wasn't a cruel master as far as slave owners go, but nobody wants to live as a slave. I met Paul in my travels and became a believer too. Then he sent me back to Philemon. He wrote a letter for me to take with me. Obeying Paul and going back was the hardest thing I have ever done. I didn't know what would happen or even if I would live through it."

"That must have taken great courage!" Vesta murmured.

"I was terrified. Philemon was angry when I first showed up. The others grabbed me and tied me to the stake in the stables while he decided what to do to me. I gave them the letter Paul had sent and then just waited. When my owner came out later, he told them to let me go. He brought me into the house, filled out papers, and gave me my freedom."

"And he had the courage after all that to ask for my freedom, too," his mother added.

"We are going to Rome. Paul has friends who will help us start a new life there," Onesimus finished.

"That's wonderful!" the girl exclaimed. "Matteo will be delighted. Paul baptized him, too. The apostle traveled on one of their ships on the way to Rome. My husband was there. He is sure that if Paul hadn't been on the ship he and his father would have drowned, as well as the whole crew."

"Amazing! Your husband was there? Is the story about the snake that bit Paul really true?"

The three were so busy talking that they didn't notice the two men from Ephesus listening to them. "Are you talking about Paul of Tarsus?" they finally asked.

Onesimus' face darkened. "Why do you want to know?" he asked suspiciously.

"Well, Paul took me with him from Ephesus when I was disowned by my family after that big riot in the temple of Diana."

The others nodded. They remembered hearing about the incident.

"He helped me find a new home, and parents to adopt me, and he raised Eutychus here back to life."

"You are the boy who fell asleep and fell out the window while Paul was preaching?" Onesimus asked incredulously.

"That would be me," the other man introduced himself.

"He still falls asleep sometimes in church," Lucas joked. Eutychus gave him a dirty look.

"Not very often," he growled. "Only when you are preaching!" It seemed as if everyone was talking at once, and the volume rose as each person spoke a little louder to be heard above the rest.

"Vesta!" Her husband grabbed her arm. "Are you all right?"

"Oh, yes! Matteo, you won't believe who these people are! It's so exciting!"

He pulled her to the side and placed himself between her and the chattering group. "It can't be as exciting as what I just found out!" he announced, grinning. "You know the sick passenger in the hold?"

"The one who is writing all the time?"

"The very one. He is John Mark—the one who wrote the stories of Jesus that the believers have been sending around. Now he travels and preaches and makes as many copies of his original scrolls as possible so more people can read them!"

"That is exciting! Do you think he will share them with us?"

"I asked him, and he says he is too sick to copy anymore anyway and that if we can find someone who can read Greek, we can read the stories all the way to Rome!" Then he lowered his voice. "I can't read Greek, can you?"

Vesta giggled. "As well as I can read any other language."

"But I think there is probably someone aboard who can."

"I can read Greek," the soft-spoken man from Lystra interrupted.

"Good," Matteo said. "And who are you?"

"I am Elihu ben Malchus."

"Your name sounds Jewish. How is it that you are from Lystra?" Matteo asked.

"I was born and raised in Jerusalem but moved to Lystra as a young man," Elihu explained briefly. "What can I read for you?"

"Oh, wait!" Vesta exclaimed, remembering what she had wanted to tell her husband. "Matteo, these people I was talking to, they all know Paul!"

"Paul?" Elihu echoed. "Paul of Tarsus, by any chance?"

"Yes, yes!" they all shouted in unison. "Our Paul!"

"Just wait till Timothy hears this!" he said.

"Timothy, the young preacher?" Lucas interrupted.

"Yes, he is down below, trying to help that poor seasick soul. I'm sure he'd much rather come up here and meet friends of Paul. Timothy has a letter from Paul he received recently. He might be willing to share that with you too."

Late into the night the group sprawled on the deck, each telling their experiences. Even the seasick John Mark felt better. During the rest of the voyage every waking minute not filled with the day-to-day work of running the ship they spent sharing what the Mighty One had done for them.

"We are all going to have to be more careful when we get to Rome," Matteo counseled one day. "Believers have been facing some persecution there now. Those who live in the city have had a hard time. Unless you have specific plans to meet someone there who can help you safely, perhaps you should come home with my wife and me, and we can assist you in making connections with the right people."

"That is kind of you," Lucas said. "But we are meeting a servant of Cornelius. He is a retired Roman centurion who—"

"Cornelius?" Vesta said with delight. "The centurion whom Peter baptized?"

"Yes. You know him?"

"No, but we've heard of him. It would be so exciting to meet him!"

"Actually, my dear," her husband whispered to her, "they are friends of my family. Their estate is not far from our home. They are wealthy believers who support the new groups springing up around Rome."

"John Mark and I would greatly appreciate your hospitality," Timothy said. "We have come to see Paul, so we will be needing to get into the city somehow. Perhaps you could aid us in getting there safely."

"There are not many believers in the actual city anymore," Matteo explained. "After the big fire that destroyed so much of Rome, the emperor blamed it on the believers. Before then many people didn't care much about us since we were members of a strange religion, but at least they didn't persecute us for that. Now the situation has changed. The believers who do live in the city are having to hide. Some of them have fled to a network of tunnels, called the catacombs, under the city. They were created as cemeteries, but now the believers hide, meet together, and even live down in them.

"It won't be easy getting to Paul. It's not like the last time he was imprisoned here. Then he was under house arrest and was a prisoner of the elite guard. Many of them became believers while he was with them. The authorities treated him well. We were able to visit him and bring him things he needed."

"Where is he now?" Lucas asked.

"The last I heard, he was in the Mamertine."

Vesta shuddered. She knew quite a bit about prisons and jails from things her father and Uncle Ari had talked about. "That's a horrible place!" she exclaimed. "My father says it is a three-level dungeon. The lower the level you are on, the less likely you are to survive."

"Poor Paul!" Onesimus remarked. "He is already old and almost blind and really arthritic from all the beatings he has received in his life. The man must be just miserable."

"Maybe not," Vesta replied. "He used to sing even when beaten so badly that he couldn't walk. Paul finds reasons to be joyful and praise God no matter what."

"That is because the joy of the Lord is his strength," Timothy commented. "Without it he would have died a long time ago."

I need to remember that, Vesta thought to herself. *If it worked for Paul and all the horrible things he has been through, it could help me. Even though feeling homesick and scared of meeting my new family isn't as important, the joy of the Lord could be my strength too.*

"I heard that Peter is imprisoned in Rome too," Lucas said. "Do you know anything about him?"

"I had not heard," Matteo answered, "but I am sure that Nero wanted him too. We need to keep both of them in our prayers. Paul is a Roman citizen, so it is technically illegal to torture him. Peter does not have that luxury."

EPILOGUE

he growing group of believers had been gathering all day, arriving in twos and threes, and discretely disappearing into the farthest winepress and harvesting area. It had ample room and shelter there and they wouldn't be seen from the road or the house. Even though Cornelius's vineyard estate was away from the city, no one could be too careful these days. Some of Paul's friends who had accompanied him back to the city had scattered after his arrest (he had told them to leave him for their own safety). The authorities rounded up others and they had not been seen since. A few just hid out of fear. The number of believers was constantly increasing, but many had died at Nero's orders.

"It's not as if we even get a respectful execution," Dion complained. "When Christians die, it's just entertainment! Something to laugh at and comment on and then go back to your dinner or whatever you were doing without a thought for the family who has lost a loved one or the friends who mourn."

Onesiphorus smiled grimly. "I guess we'd still be just as dead even if it was a 'respectful execution.'"

Antonia and her servants had carefully smuggled bread and fruit out to the hiding place earlier that day. "Please," Cornelius said, "please find a spot and make yourselves comfortable. I'm sorry we don't have a banquet room to offer you. Well, actually we do, but I'm sure we all feel safer out here."

Many in the group nodded. Cornelius raised his hand and offered thanks for their safety and the food they were going to share, then asked God's blessing on the group, those who were not with them, and especially Peter and Paul.

"I know you are all hungry for news, and tonight we have more than usual, but I want to honor our Savior, Jesus—Yeshua for our Jewish brothers and sisters—before we hear it all." Cornelius picked up a piece of flat bread that had been baked that afternoon. Each believer did the same. "In the night He was betrayed, Jesus took bread, and when he had given thanks He broke it and said, 'This is My body; do this in remembrance of Me.'" Cornelius closed his eyes and placed the piece of bread in his mouth. The others did the same.

Antonia felt tears gathering behind her closed eyelids. "I remember You, Yeshua," she whispered. "How could I ever forget You? You've been so good to us." Without thinking she ran her hand down over her swollen belly. Even though she was getting pretty old for it, the Lord was still blessing her and Cornelius with children.

She smiled as she thought of the early years of their marriage. They had just had Portia, and then nothing for what seemed forever. And yet the Lord had blessed them with children when Cornelius' years of duty were over and they were ready for him to retire and move back to Rome. "I'm glad I am so much younger than the husband You gave me," she whispered. "Otherwise you'd be doing Sarah-type miracles at our house. I just wish I had been able to know You when You were in Judea."

Cornelius raised one of the few silver cups. "I'm sorry we don't have many cups out here. But if we were disturbed and needed to flee into the vineyard, we wouldn't want to leave evidence." The others understood. "Jesus said, 'This is My blood that was spilled for you. As often as you do this, you will show that you remember Me and My death till I come.'" He handed the cups to his waiting friends, and each one took a sip and passed it on.

To Dion it had seemed a little strange the first time he saw the believers do this, but after he traveled with Paul and met so many Jews it made perfect sense. Sin could not be blotted out without the shedding of blood. Jesus' death and His blood made it so that from then on no one had to sacrifice a lamb to be forgiven for each sin. Jesus had paid for all of them with His blood. He had even paid in advance for people such as Dion, and anyone else who became believers later on. It still amazed him, even though he had heard it many times now. He couldn't think of any other religion in which the god involved loved humans at all, much less so passionately that he would rather give His own life than to give up His people.

"Yeshua," Dion whispered, "there is just no one like You. You are amazing. And I love You. I think You are the only one who truly loved me until Priscilla and Aquila." The old empty place in his chest started to hurt again. He tried not to think about his parents—and he was getting better at it—but the pain was still in there, aching and slipping out when he was trying to concentrate on something else.

"Now," Cornelius announced, "we have several in our midst who arrived in Rome a few weeks ago. We have been unable to get together safely until now, so we have lots of news from faraway places to share with you. Onesiphorus has been in to see Paul and Peter this week, and he will update us on them. For those of you who are hungry for things other than news, there is lots of bread and dried fruit in these baskets. Those of you who need it, please take as much as you need. There are some cheeses in that other basket. Please feel free to help yourselves as we talk."

Lucas grinned at Dion. "I know what you're hungry for, and it isn't food or news," he whispered. His friend blushed.

"Don't be silly," Dion said.

"I'm not silly. And I'm not blind. I've never seen your eyes follow anyone like that before."

Dion elbowed Lucas in the ribs. "Hush and get some of Antonia's wonderful pastries before I have to eat your share. Anyway, there is no law against thinking the daughter of Cornelius is beautiful. Even believers can recognize that fact."

Lucas chuckled. "But she has to be one of the most spirited girls among the believers. Whoever takes her as a wife will not have the traditional life they expected."

Dion said nothing. He had never expected such a life anyway. And he had never planned to marry any girl. Families just caused a lot of pain, and it was something he never intended to be a part of again. Still, the two weeks he and Lucas had stayed at Cornelius' home had been amazing. His thoughts and feelings were now all tangled up. And Portia was not like any other woman he had ever met. So far he had just admired her from across the room. Whenever she was present he couldn't think of anything to say, and he wasn't sure he should anyway. He was having trouble sleeping at night, and when he did finally drift off, he dreamed of his mother. That hadn't happened for a long time. Eating pastries was definitely better than trying to figure it out tonight.

"Eutychus and his brother Lucas come to us from Ephesus." Cornelius continued. "What is the news there?"

"The apostle John sends his love and encouragement to all of you here near Rome," Eutychus said. "The church in Ephesus is doing well and growing. Many of us are taking short missionary trips as our responsibilities allow, and the church cares for our families when we do. Yeshua's mother is becoming elderly but is still living with John and his family, just as Yeshua requested before He died. We came to Rome not only as part of our mission trip, but also to express our support to Paul and brother Peter. Even if we cannot see them face to face, we want them to know we are here and praying for them." He sat down to murmured "Amens."

"Lucas?" Cornelius asked.

"Eutychus said everything I was going to say," he commented with a grin. "I have to wait until he dozes off to get any words in sideways!" The group laughed. Even though it had happened when Eutychus was only a boy, he was always known as the one who fell asleep in church and died when he fell out of a window. The prayers of Paul had brought the power of the Lord to resurrect him. It was a story that Eutychus was a little tired of hearing but tolerated with good humor.

He nudged Lucas in the ribs. "For an adopted brother, you are almost as annoying as a real one," he whispered.

"Onesimus and his mother come to us from Ephesus too," Cornelius said. "Some of you will remember him from his visit with us about a year ago. At that time he was a fugitive slave. This time he comes to us with all the dignity of a freedman—and a freed mother, too." Everyone clapped and praised the Lord.

"I am so grateful to those of you who were so kind to me last year. You treated me with dignity as if I were one of you. I was afraid, and you gave me encouragement. I was hungry, and you fed me. I had nothing, and you gave me shelter, and when I gathered up my courage to obey Paul and return to my master, you gave me everything I needed for my trip home. Many now treat me with respect as a freedman, but I will always hold you who were so good to me even when I was a slave in my heart as . . . as . . ." Tears welled up in his eyes.

Cornelius put his arm around Onesimus. "The ground is level at the foot of Jesus' cross," he said. "And all of us were slaves in one respect or another. All of us deserve very little but receive respect because we are His, and to love Him is to treat His friends with love too."

Onesimus nodded and wiped his face on his sleeve. He glanced at his mother. Her eyes were streaming with tears, but when he smiled at her she just looked away. His mother was the saddest person he knew. For a while he had thought becoming free would have helped, but she still seemed lost in a faraway pain that he could not reach or understand.

"Meanwhile, Timothy and Eli ben Malchus come to us from Lystra," Cornelius continued.

"Isn't that the place that stoned Paul and Barnabas?" someone asked.

"Yes," the retired centurion responded quickly as the room began to buzz with voices. "But out of that also came the great young preacher Timothy, whom Paul spent a lot of time mentoring and grooming for leadership."

"Isn't the Malchus family from Jerusalem? Aren't they highly connected with the high priest's family?" one person questioned.

"I thought it was one of them whom Peter chopped the ear off that night in the garden," another commented.

Cornelius held his hand up to get their attention. "Yes, these things are true. Jesus healed Malchus's ear. Eli ben Malchus had to leave Jerusalem during the persecution. He and his mother have been believers from the beginning. These are known stories, and Eli is not a spy among us. How is your family now, Eli?"

"My mother is well. When my father died in Jerusalem, I brought her to Lystra with my cousin Timothy's family. Timothy's father has also died, so Timothy and I care for our mothers and our grandmother Lois. Except for this trip, we alternate our travel schedules so there is always someone at home."

The gathered believers indicated their approval. "I recently received another letter from Paul," Timothy said. "It seemed to be his last words to us, and I have been traveling and sharing it with believers everywhere I could. I think it will be very encouraging to them, especially if they . . . um . . . you know, if Paul is . . ."

"Yes," Cornelius intervened as Timothy struggled for words. "If that happens, we will all need encouragement, and sharing Paul's letter is a wonderful idea. Perhaps you will read it to us later tonight?"

Timothy swallowed hard and nodded. The idea of anything happening to his beloved mentor Paul was hard to think about even as a possibility. However would he cope if it actually happened? He wished God would take Paul to heaven in a blaze of glory or a fiery chariot like the prophet Elijah. That would set those Roman guards back a peg or two. Then he sighed. Those Roman guards were probably the very reason God would *not* intervene. It seemed that many of Paul's guards through the years had become some of the most devout believers. The Lord loved the guards, too. But Timothy still wished things could be different for his beloved old friend.

Cornelius was speaking again. "Physician Luke is with us tonight too. He has been a traveling companion to Paul for many of his journeys and is working on something you will want to hear about."

"As most of you know," Luke began, "I have attended Paul and his friends for many years." He received nods of recognition from others in the group. "I know many of you believe that all illness and pain are sent by God to punish humans for things they have done wrong. I do not think that is what Jesus taught, but I don't want to debate that point tonight. Through the years I have kept a journal of the stories we heard from people who knew Yeshua, and also accounts of Paul's adventures as His missionary. I have divided them into the stories about Jesus and the stories about the work of the apostles since then."

"But John Mark has already written a book about Jesus," someone protested.

"Are you saying his book was inaccurate and yours is better?" another demanded.

"How can your book be better? You didn't even know Jesus. At least John Mark did."

"Stop! Stop!" Cornelius commanded. "Most of us have heard the stories from Mark's book, and they are wonderful. For people like me who never had the opportunity to travel with Him and sit at His feet, there will never be too many stories of Him available to me. The more the better. John Mark's story is an eyewitness account. Luke's story is a collection of experiences from many eyewitnesses. We will all be the richer for having more available to us."

Several in the group nodded. Another man stood to his feet. "I am John Mark," he said. "And I am delighted for Dr. Luke to be writing stories too. There are not enough books in the world to record all the things Yeshua did when He was here. I am also really happy that he has recorded the experiences of Paul. Paul has written many letters to others, but not his own life story. The more accounts we have of the way God has cared for those who believe in His Son, the more we will be encouraged to keep the faith—especially in hard times."

He stopped and gave a little chuckle. "In the early days when I first traveled with Paul, I was supposed to be recording his sermons to send out to the other churches. Instead I wrote the life of Jesus. We were both frustrated with each other." He smiled. "But here we are years later, and I have more respect for Paul than any man on earth, and he likes my book. The body of Christ has an important place for each one of us, and as a part of one body we also learn to love each other. It's hard to imagine now that at one time many believers disliked Paul. That they were willing to let him worship Yeshua—just not with them!"

A ripple of surprise spread among some of the newer believers. "Yet now," John Mark continued, "we are all gathered here because we love Paul, and even though we can't be with him we are as close as we can get to offer encouragement!"

"This is our friend, Onesiphorus," Cornelius announced. "He is the only one who has figured out how to visit our brothers Peter and Paul safely."

"Things don't look good," Onesiphorus said bluntly. "Both of our brothers are in poor health, and I fear that even if their executions were not planned so soon they would be nearing their ends anyway. The official in charge told me they are both to die tomorrow."

A moan of sorrow raced through the assembled group; then it fell silent. "Do we know how?" Cornelius asked.

Onesiphorus nodded. "It sounds," he began, "as if both executions will be private. Even though few Christians remain in Rome, Nero is a little concerned there might be too much support for them. Because Paul is a citizen, he will be beheaded. But since Peter is Jewish, they are planning a crucifixion."

"Is there anything we can do?" Lucas said.

"Just pray, encourage each other, and keep our eyes on Jesus. Paul is in good spirits, though he is so crippled from his arthritis he can hardly move. He said not being able to see well has been an advantage in this situation.

"My friend Onesimus lent me his mother as part of my disguise. Paul was greatly encouraged to find out that Philemon had granted Onesimus his freedom as a result of the letter he had written."

Many believers nodded and patted Onesimus on the back. But Dion was busy looking at Portia again. The girl was talking to someone beside her. It was hard not to eavesdrop when he was sitting right behind them.

"You saw Paul?" Portia breathlessly asked the heavily veiled woman beside her.

"He was amazing!" the person next to her said. "Although he looked terrible he sounded so positive. Paul said that he had run his race and fought his fight and was looking forward to receiving his crown. They may chop off his head, but I doubt they'll get the smile off his face. It's almost as if he's looking forward to the execution."

Dion scooted a little closer and tried to appear as if he weren't listening.

"What changed my whole life," the woman continued, "was our visit with Peter. He looked badly treated and was in tears most of the time we were together. In the beginning he kept repeating how he had betrayed Jesus that night, and that he wasn't worthy to receive the same punishment that our Lord had. Then he started asking questions about my faith. I told him I could not believe the gracious gift of salvation was available to me after what had happened in my life."

Portia put her arms around the woman. "Whatever it was, the Lord will forgive you. And Peter would too."

A sob shook the woman's shoulders. "My story is a lot like Peter's," she said, "except that I turned my back on my own son. I should have tried to save him, but I couldn't say or do a thing. I felt so powerless, so I just stood there in silence as my husband sold him into the most miserable life I could imagine. I don't see how my son could ever forgive me and—and—I'll never be able to forgive myself. I'm sure he suffered terribly, and I hope he never lived to become a man."

Dion could hardly breathe. The old pain in his chest had grown into a clawed monster that wanted to burst out of him.

"But Peter said," she continued to sob, her words barely understandable, "that the Lord had forgiven me a long time ago and that now I needed to forgive myself. Then he prayed and asked God to give me a sign that I'd been forgiven. Peter was so kind to me! And he seemed to be encouraged himself as we talked about how forgiving the Lord is."

Dion couldn't keep quiet any more. He tapped the woman on the shoulder. "What was your son's name?"

"His name was Dion," she replied.

He began to tingle from head to toe. Could it be? After all these years? Could it be her?

"Mother?" he asked.

"Dion?" she shrieked.

He flung his arms around her.

"What is going on here?" Onesimus demanded, noticing the commotion. "And take your hands off my mother!"

"My name is Dion, and she is my mother," he replied, not letting go.

"Yes! Yes!" his mother gasped for breath. "Onesimus, this is your brother Dion!"

"I don't understand!" Onesimus sputtered. "We were slaves to Philemon, but who is he?"

His mother reached out and drew him into the circle. "I wasn't always a slave," she said. "When your father and I were first married we were free. But your father fell ill and drank too much. He was always sorry the next day, but he drank everything he earned. And he sold us to help pay his debts."

"He sold you, too?" Dion sputtered in disbelief. "How could I not forgive you when he sold you, too?"

"I was sold to Philemon as a house slave. But you were sold to that evil man. All those years it was torture knowing how you suffered. I hoped that you had died and been spared the pain."

Dion broke into a smile. "Mother, don't torture yourself any more. I have the most wonderful story to tell you! I escaped after only a week! The Lord heard your prayers and took wonderful care of me!"

"Wait!" Cornelius interrupted. "Tell all of us." Still holding his mother with one arm, Dion moved to the center of the group and began to speak.

I smiled. Sharing accounts of the Mighty One's goodness and love is exactly what His people are to be doing during times of stress. After all, their strength comes from their joy in Him. The excited storytelling continued through the night. The sun was just peeking over the hillside as Cornelius called the group to order.

"Friends, morning is upon us. Today we will say goodbye to our precious friends Peter and Paul. But having heard all the glorious things God has done in their lives and that of so many others, let's not mourn, but rejoice in what the Lord has done with these men. Timothy, perhaps you can read us a little of Paul's letter again before we have to leave."

Standing, Timothy pulled out his parchment. "My life is being given as an offering to God, and the time has come for me to leave this life. I have fought the good fight, I have finished the race, I have kept the faith. Now, a crown is being held for me—a crown for being right with God. The Lord, the judge who judges rightly, will give me the crown on that day—not only to me but to all those who have waited with love for him to come again" (2 Timothy 4:6-8, NCV).

After a brief prayer, the believers melted into the vineyard. It was not safe for all of them to be seen leaving at once. The guardians and warriors, though unseen, accompanied them, each person embarking on a new adventure. I and several others were allowed to enter Rome and witness the final minutes of the lives of two of the Mighty One's human friends. Both of them met their ends with anticipation of spending eternity with Him.

As I thought of all the human arguments about what happens when a person dies I smiled to myself. And while the believers in this group buried their loved ones in the ground and knew they slept until the time when all God's friends would be raised for His great final triumph, I knew something more. Time is a human thing. To those who are dead there is no time. So to the living, the dead may wait a long time, but to the dead it seems instantaneous. To Paul it would seem that just as the executioner tensed for that final blow, Jesus would appear in all His glory and catch Paul up with Him. And for Peter, just as he felt that he could bear no more and that his life was seeping out his wounds, there would be his Lord! And his pain would be over. Humans can get so confused. It would be so much easier just to trust Him.

Today the believers could mourn or shout in victory, or a little of both. But their strength is in His joy! His people are so precious to Him, to be carefully nurtured and gently saved from further pain so that He can present them to His Father in triumph and delight! Who could turn down such a life? Not Peter. Not Paul. Not Vesta or Priscilla. Not Eutychus and not Lucas. What about you?

THE ACTION-PACKED STORIES OF THE GATES SERIES

You won't be able to put down these stories of suspense and surprise, battle and captivity, kings and tragedy. They sound like make-believe, but they aren't: these are the enthralling, often forgotten stories of the Old Testament—told as you've never heard them before.

Siege at the Gates
The Story of Sennacherib, Hezekiah, and Isaiah
Paperback, 157 pages.
978-0-8127-0441-9

Fire in the Gates
The Story of Baruch, Jeremiah, and Nebuchadnezzar
Paperback, 107 pages.
978-0-8127-0443-3

The Temple Gates
The Story of Josiah, Jedidah, and Judah's Idolatry
Paperback, 144 pages.
978-0-8127-0442-6

Gate of the Gods
The Story of Daniel, Nebuchadnezzar, and Loyalty to God
Paperback, 128 pages.
978-0-8127-0444-0

The Open Gates
The Story of Cyrus, Daniel, and Darius
Paperback, 176 pages.
978-0-8127-0445-7

FAMILY BIBLE STORY
SERIES

O ne of the most extensively researched Bible story books on the market today, this series offers features which give background information to engage every member of the family, young and old alike. Written by Ruth Redding Brand and illustrated by distinguished artists, these carefully researched and beautifully illustrated books will make Bible characters come alive for your children. Every name, place, and custom is carefully explained. Hardcover. Available individually or as a set.

Abraham, 109 pages. ISBN 0-8280-1856-1
Adam & Eve, 95 pages. ISBN 0-8280-1850-2
Jacob, 127 pages. ISBN 0-8280-1852-9
Joseph, 87 pages. ISBN 0-8280-1854-5

REVIEW AND HERALD®
PUBLISHING ASSOCIATION

OTHER EXCITING STORIES
IN THE FAMILY FAVORITES SERIES

THESE WATCHED HIM DIE
Leslie Hardinge
They were there that day—
they saw Jesus die. And
these are their stories.
Paperback.

THE SWORD OF DENIS ANWYCK
Maylan Schurch
NEW! Paperback.

THE GATES SERIES
by Thurman C. Petty, Jr.

SIEGE AT THE GATES
The Story of Sennacherib,
Hezekiah, and Isaiah
Paperback, 160 pages.

THE TEMPLE GATES
The Story of Josiah,
Jedidah, and Judah's Idolatry
Paperback, 144 pages.

FIRE IN THE GATES
The Story of Nebuchadnezzar,
Jeremiah, and Baruch
Paperback, 112 pages.

GATE OF THE GODS
The Story of Daniel, Nebuchadnezzar,
and Loyalty to God
Paperback, 128 pages.

THE OPEN GATES
The Story of Cyrus, Daniel, and Darius
Paperback, 176 pages.